15 LESSONS

OR LESSONS IN LIVING

FROM THE PRINCIPLES OF CREATION TO THE PRINCIPLES OF HEALTH AND PROSPERITY

ELIZABETH TOWNE

CONTENTS

.

INTRODUCTION.

IN this book I design to state in logical and practical form the new philosophy of life and living. To do this I must stick closely to a clear statement of the philosophy itself, without trying to give you too many proofs. It might take seventy lectures to reason you into accepting the new view of life; and still you would be unconvinced.

Why? Because reason is an endless labyrinth out of which no man emerges unaided by a higher wisdom than itself. Reason is the original Chinese puzzle, forever unsolved until you get up above reason; up above the labyrinth and look down upon it to see where you are going. The walls, and walls within walls, of reason's labyrinth are your prejudices.

No man climbs over a prejudice; he merely seeks the first opening around it, and finds himself in another alley of the labyrinth! The only way to know a blind alley before you see it, the only way to know your own prejudice-wall when you see it, is to go up in a balloon and look down.

Once admit that there is a way to get above reason, that there is an intelligence above reason, in which reason lives and moves and by which it expands and grows, and you find yourself already mounting and looking over the walls of those blind alleys of reason that lead into more blind alleys. If you keep on looking down on reason you will eventually raze many of its prejudice walls, that serve no purpose except to cut off the view of life as a whole.

"A narrow mind" is a most expressive term; it exactly describes the mind whose energy flows between endless prejudice-walls that merely shut off its view of larger things, while it wanders endlessly in mental alleys that lead to more mental alleys, weariness, death.

These prejudice-alleys—common to all mankind—are alleys built through reasoning by the light of the five physical senses only. Not until man finds these inadequate and turns away yearning for a satisfaction never found, does he realize that after all there may be more to life than he has seen, smelt, felt, heard, or tasted. Then he looks up from his mental alleys and glimpses— PRINCIPLE, instead of things; God above and in things, instead of man alone, inadequate.

"He that cometh unto God must believe that he is, and that he is a rewarder of them that diligently seek him."

Perhaps there may be some who cannot get away from their prejudices long enough to really catch the new view of life. Let us take a hint from Shakespeare, then, and play pretend. "If all the world's a stage" and we are players, let us choose to lay aside our old parts while we read these pages, and let us take up the new part of the new thought philosophy, forgetting the old and putting into the new all the imagination and will and interest at our command.

Let us assume a philosophy if we have it not.

Let us play pretend, like children. Only as little children can we enter a new heaven and transformed life.

1

THE FOUNDATION OF LIFE.

ALL our Darwins and Huxleys and Haeckels have come at the last to agree that back of all living forms, and back of the first amoeba itself, there is Something that eye and microscope and scalpel cannot cope with; a something that informs everything, animate and inanimate, without which that thing cannot be formed or held together.

This Something the scientist proves and affirms, but refuses to define. The religionist tries to define it, but fails to prove its existence or its nature.

The scientist says, "I cannot see, hear, smell, taste, or feel this Something, therefore I do not know what it is, and nothing is worth counting except what can be known."

The religionist says, "I see there is a Something that moves at the heart of all nature including man; this Something must be very mighty, therefore I will find out its will and work with it; I will beseech It to enlighten me and lead me."

So the scientist digs through things and finds God; while the religionist aspires above things and finds God—one God, the life of all life, and more.

What is God, the First Cause, the Life, the Prime Mover in all creation? "God is Love," says the Good Book. "God is Mind," "God is Principle," God is Life," "God is Spirit," "God is Soul."

Alexander Pope says all creation is "one stupendous Whole, whose body nature is, and God the soul." And again, "From the soule the bodye forme doth take."

In plain words, God is the primal substance that fills all space, all time; out of which and by which all things are made.

The nature of God is mind. The mode of motion of universal mind is thought. God thought or spoke the universe into being, and God is still thinking this universe into greater being; thinking in and through you and me, and through all the lower forms of life as well.

I think it is logical—and maybe safe! —to say that God cannot think except through you and me; that all the thought he has is your thought and mine, the thought of all the forms of life that are or have been, in this world and in all worlds.

God by his thought is proving himself, and he has not proved as yet more than the sum of the thought of all peoples and worlds. God is thinking out a great inspiration of his, and the universe is his organized thought.

God's thought forms are all temporary, ever changing from better to best. But God himself is absolute, the same yesterday, today, and forever. But mind is only God's character. Back of that is something else which is himself, his being, his essence, his ABSOLUTE substance.

In character, God is Mind; in essence, he is Love. Back of thinking lies LOVE, SPIRIT, SOUL; and the thinking that fails to take this universal love-spirit, soul, into every counsel is very narrow, shortsighted, and inadequate thinking indeed.

"God is love" goes back to the absolute, eternal, omnipresent TRUTH of all being, the prime mover of all doing. God is love, and love is twofold, made up of equal parts of will and wisdom. Will is active or positive; wisdom is receptive or negative. Will corresponds to the male principle of all creation, wisdom to the female. One expands and projects; the other conserves. In every tiny atom and ion and corpuscle of life these two principles inhere. Without the two of them there would never have been a beginning of creation.

In the ultimate there is but one dual principle of life, male and female, will and wisdom, inherent in every atom and in every organism of life, in every thought of every mind: "Male and female created he them"—not male or female.

Among the forms of life, every masculine is feminine within, and every feminine is masculine within. Because of this is the everlasting attraction between the two.

A perfect balance of this dual principle in any organism would result in separation from its fellows, the hermit life of uselessness to society as a whole. This is illustrated in mineral life by a slight experiment. Take a bar of magnetized iron. One end is negative, the other positive. Cut it into pieces. The pieces, each of which has its positive and negative poles, will adhere to each other. But turn the middle piece around, bringing two positives together, and you cannot make them stick.

Magnetize two needles and place them with positive poles together, and they will instantly fly apart. Turn one needle the other end about, and they will cling together. Thus attraction works, always, between positive and negative, male and female, light and dark, will and wisdom.

Will, the male principle of life, is electric, positive in its action. It is the centrifugal force that throws off energy, as the sun throws off rays and worlds. Wisdom, the female principle, is magnetic, attractive, negative, the centripetal force of nature that draws together and binds, as the earth draws the sun's electric rays, as the matrix draws, holds, conserves the seed. It is the magnetic centripetal force that balances the sun's electric, radiating, projecting power.

These two forces are inherent in every atom and ion and corpuscle of the universe; in every thought of the universe.

Now go back to the beginning of things and imagine the state of space— full of Love, Mind, God; full of unformed thought— thought (or corpuscles; they are one) diffused like vapor; all the corpuscles or thoughts exactly alike, held equidistant from each other by equal action of the electric and magnetic forces inherent in each; all whirling on their axes and in their orbits, just as worlds whirl to-day.

Then God, Love, the Will-and-Wisdom One, moved upon the face of the deep to organize these corpuscles into Ideas. God wanted a kaleidoscope for his amusement! He grew a bit tired of the sameness of his thought, as it were; and a wave of relaxation, of cooling, went over the face of the deep, which disturbed the equilibrium of electric and magnetic corpuscles. They began to draw together in little nuclei, in little nebulous patches, closer and closer in spots, separating from other congregations of corpuscles, just as described in the nebular hypothesis of creation.

When the first two corpuscles (or thoughts) approached in space, creation or living organization began. Here we get our first view of the wonderful Seven Principles of Creation, without which nothing was made that was made; the seven principles inherent in every little electric-magnetic, male-and female corpuscle in all time and space; inherent in every living thing that has yet appeared, including man and the spirits or mahatmas, if there are such; the seven principles by which God creates, the same seven principles by which you and I create and re-create. God thought this universe into being all by himself, until he had completed up to and including man. He thought man- out in his own image and likeness, so that man might think with him, work with him, in all creating to come. Man is God's Idea; and God's Ideas are working together in and with him—by those same old seven principles—to create greater glories than either God or man has yet dreamed over; greater than God or man could possibly accomplish alone.

You are God's thought-child, and your ideas are God's grandchildren, as it were!

This is your genealogy!—don't get yourself mixed up in earth heredity. As Ella Wheeler Wilcox sings:— "Back of thy parents and thy grandparents lies the great eternal Will; That, too, is thine inheritance; strong, beautiful, divine; sure lever of success for him who tries."

And father, sons, and grandsons are all working together on one Big Job— the job of making a new heaven and a new earth, a bigger, brighter, better heaven and earth for the joy of all; a heaven and earth that shall prove the dream God dreamed before .he ever began to think at all.

2

THE SEVEN PRINCIPLES OF CREATION.

NOW back to our seven principles by which God thinks out a creation; by which you and I are governed; by which OUR THOUGHTS are governed in their action on further creation of ourselves and our environments. First, remember that the dual principle of all life, the essence of God and you, Will and Wisdom (male and female, electric and magnetic), is indivisible, inseparable, omnipresent, omnipotent, omniscient. It is one as the two tight-twisted strands of a rope are one—one strand uppermost and active at this point, the other at the next, but both of them fully present and indivisible.

The seven principles are the inherent laws by which will and wisdom work out creation. These, too, may be likened to a rope, a seven-strand, seven colored, tight-twisted one, where each strand comes uppermost in turn, each in its turn dominating and giving color to the whole.

These seven principles work alike in every tiniest corpuscle, ion, and atom of the universe; they govern the forming and the whirling of worlds; they manifest in their entirety in the lowest forms of vegetable life, as well as in the highest forms of the animal and the human.

The same seven principles govern in the founding, perpetuation, and disintegration of the family, the society, secret or otherwise, the school, town, state, government, the world itself. Wherever there is atom, thought, or organization, be it microscopic or telescopic, mineral, plant, animal, human, superhuman, there the seven principles are active. Let one of these principles get lazy on its job, and all creation and imagination itself would stand still with the shock.

The seven principles by which God creates are as everywhere present as God himself. Not even "the idle word" is so small that the whole seven principles are not fully active within it. Do you get that?

And do you get the truth that God is in his world as well as in his heaven; that all "matter" is thought; and that in every thought atom and organization of atoms inhere the seven creative principles of life by which God-in-us organizes and grows things?

1. First among the seven principles is Force; power, with its color a strong, crude red. The reds of nature show where all the principles inhere with the first one, force, uppermost. The family or person dominated by this principle is rough, rude, forceful above wisdom, and you will often find him housed in red buildings, wearing red clothing, frequently tearing around in red rages; believing in hell fire and the rod and doing his part toward feeding the one and exercising the other.

These same people are not at all devoid of love or sense or wisdom; they are merely dominated for the time by the first of the seven principles, just as sharp-cornered, solid red rocks are dominated by forces.

Force, the first principle, draws things together and holds them there. If force were the only principle, creation might be a ragged red rock; or perhaps a red rock sphere.

2. But here comes in Discrimination, the second principle, with its color of delicate pink. It shows up somewhat in our red family, but its positive qualities are underneath, as Ideals and longings that the family wants to realize but can't quite. The family or person in whom discrimination is uppermost is very dainty; affects delicate colors, high art, and a die-away voice; abhors crude-art; despises business, brawn, and force; and is critical and fault-finding generally. Such a person may possess all sorts of

virtues, but his life is colored and dominated by the second principle, discrimination.

First, life draws atoms and people together; second, it discriminates, holding this atom or person, rejecting that. 3. Next Life arranges the atoms or persons it has drawn together. Here comes the third principle, Order, its color pale blue. Who has not seen the family where order dominates, where everything is done exactly the same every day, comfort sacrificed to system, with the very atmosphere blue? The person whose positive choice of color is pale blue is almost sure to be one in whom the principle of order is dominant.

In the lower forms of life order is rarely the dominant principle, so even blue flowers are scarce. We look up to find the blues, in the skies, on the distant hills, in man's eyes—"the windows of his soul." In man's works we find order and its blue coming of tener to the surface.

The color blue is attributed to wisdom, and Butler seems to identify wisdom and order. This seems to me like saying God and order are one, but God and force, or God and cohesion, are less one; for wisdom and will (or God) include all the seven principles equally; or so it seems to me. Order is only one of wisdom's principles of action. The rainbow is the color of wisdom! Let us leave blue to the principle of order. For some of the ideas expressed in chapters 2, 3 and 4, I am indebted to Butler's "Seven Creative Principles."

3
NATURE'S DEVIL.

WITH our last chapter we left creation in good order, with the third principle of nature, order, in possession, and everything showing a clear blue. If life itself had taken a vacation with us, we should have seen twenty-four hours of such blues as no one has dreamed. No change anywhere, just a world vibrating to the tone of order, sky blue; a universe of blue, bas-relief against a blue sky! Happily all the seven principles kept on working while we played. To re-state:— First, there is Force, the first principle, the principle of attraction, that draws things, atoms, worlds, and people together.

Helen Wihnans called God the Law of Attraction, but you will readily see that this is a misnomer, as the law of attraction is only one of the seven principles by which God creates. God by any name would be the same, and Helen Wilmans' name for him does not spoil the splendid thinking-out which she did for this day and age. But her statement should not hold us from thinking still farther.

By the way, the color of force is red. Helen Wilmans was impressed with the force or attraction side of life, and I am told that in hair and complexion she showed the sandy reds that belong to that principle; just an interesting illustration of the way these principles of life crop out in what is commonly called "coincidence." Second comes in the principle of Discrimination, which decides what shall be attracted and what let alone. Third comes Order, deciding where each thing shall be placed.

Then comes the work of the fourth principle:—

4. After drawing atoms or people together, discriminating as to quality, arranging in order, Life next binds them in one organization. Thus comes in the fourth principle of life, Cohesion, the color of green that we see in the spring. To the person

dominated by cohesion, green is a favorite color and any change is a horror. To keep things as they are seems to him the chief end of life. The attic is full of old stuff he can't let go of. His coffers are full of cash and his head of old fogy ideas. He is clannish; his daughters and sons are run into the same mold with father and mother. Green-eyed jealousy stands guard against innovation.

Cohesion means family ties as distinct from family progress. Unhappy the son and daughter of the house of ties!

5. Unless they are alive enough to kick, to will for themselves, to raise a ferment in the family and release themselves to follow their ideals. Ideals are the yeast that makes active the fifth principle of life, Fermentation. This principle is the real devil of all history, all mythology, of Christianity itself. It is the destroying principle of life that comes in to tear down that which has served its purpose and must give way to better things.

The college boy goes back to the tiebound home and raises the devil of a ferment that causes much pain, but eventually releases them all to more life, further growth.

Fermentation is the death principle that acts on all forms of life not fit to be perpetuated. It is dominant in the actinic or destroying rays of the sun that cause decomposition. Its color is deep indigo blue, or black—the color of mourning, pain, loss (of the old), death. The family in which this principle is dominant is the family of mourning, darkened rooms, black clothing, secret sorrows, losses and crosses, troubles, tribulations, and death.

Not because this principle is really any more painful in its action than any other of the seven, but because man fights it harder. We find ourselves living on the surface of life, judging from appearances, and resisting change. The resistance is due to the activity of the first principle, force. Force holds together, fermentation separates. But there is no real reason why the action of either principle should give us pain.

There is no reason or cause for the pain accompanying change and death, except in the individual mind. It is "all in your mind";

not at all in any inherent quality or principle of nature or life itself, but in unnatural resistance of the individual mind, governed by false concepts of life.

Do you doubt this? Then tell me why one man courts death while another abhors it. Why does one woman feel only peaceful relief at the death of a very aged and infirm relative, while another in similar condition grieves herself sick over it? Why is one person frightened at the thing another enjoys?

Why does one man joy in travel while his neighbor hates it? Why does one hate the taste of cod liver oil while his brother likes it? Why do you "turn against" things you once liked?

The mental attitude governs in every case; and your mental attitude is determined by your concepts of things in particular and of life in general. If you really believed what Spiritualists claim to believe about the death of a child, could you be anything but happy that a child had died and escaped the miseries and uncertainties of life on earth?

Your feelings of resistance to anything are roused by your belief in evil. I am showing you that there is no evil; that life is an orderly creation progressing by interaction of seven beneficent principles. If you can catch this concept—if you are ready for it— you will pass out forever from the old realm of sin, sickness, death, pain.

4

TRANSMUTATION OF EVIL.

HERE comes in the sixth principle of life, Transmutation. Fermentation is full of purpose. It disintegrates the useless and makes it ready for transmutation to higher forms. Out of the fermenting swamp rises the lily. Out of hard experience and suffering comes wisdom. Out of disappointed personal love comes universal love and world-helping.

Whitman's heart fermented, disintegrated, nearly broke over an unrequited love; by and by he saw that love is for the lover and the world; and out of it all came forth his immortal poems. Every great man and woman has paralleled Whitman's experience.

The lesser love ferments and out of it rises the greater love for all mankind. The family itself disintegrates that the race may gain.

This is what Jesus meant when he said one must forsake family loves, houses, and lands for the kingdom's sake. To hold family loves against the race, to devote all one's self to personal loves, is to invite disintegration. To cherish the family love as a part of the race love is to keep it. One does not know how to love a person well and happily unless he first loves all persons. Fermentation comes into one's life to lighter it and make room for greater things, for greater joys and loves, for fuller usefulness and wisdom. Fermentation is John the Baptist to Transmutation, which is Christ before the resurrection.

Nothing goes out of a life but to make room for something better.

To let things go, instead of resisting and grieving over the change, is to work with the underlying wisdom and will of life. "Resignation to God's will" is the key to peaceful and normal growth. Kicking against change only makes gnarls and scars, and side-tracks energy from one's life business of growing.

Transmutation, the sixth principle of life, brings reorganization and glory. Its color is the clear purple of the passion flower. It is full of passion, fire, activity. The person in whom transmutation happens to be dominant is moved to think outside the ordinary channels. He comes out and is separate in thought, at least, from the fashions of his mental and physical environment.

He forsakes old habits of thought and sets his face toward a larger view of life. The new thought movement is a transmutation movement, its people dominated for the time by the transmutation principle.

7. But there is still another principle of life, the principle of Sensation, blessing, its color the clear yellow of the sun.

"While in itself sensation is a distinct principle, yet, without its alliance to matter, to organism, there is no sensation. Sensation is a mode of consciousness."

Sensation is that which results from the impingement of etheric waves upon an organism built up by interaction of the first six principles of life. Sensation takes possession of the organism, so to speak, and uses it for its own.

Just what sensation is like no scientist has dared to say. It is one of those eternal substances that we cannot see, hear, smell, taste, or feel; but without it there could be no seeing, tasting, smelling, hearing, or feeling.

As nearly as I can sense sensation, it is God; God reaching out through all senses and getting acquainted with his ideas, and steering his ideas (you and me, you know) into safe paths, paths of usefulness, peace, and blessing.

Every organized being moves in a sea of vibrations, and by reaching out toward them, by aspiring toward them, he works with the vibrations to build the organs through which those vibrations are registered. Ears and eyes, noses and feelers, are all marconigraphs.

Every atom, cell, and corpuscle in your body is a Marconi station for catching spiritual or etheric vibrations on its own account, and for the good of you as a whole.

And the more highly organized your body is the greater the range of vibrations it can register for the use of this spiritual substance-life called sense.

The expression "five senses" is not scientific from any point of view. Looking at it from the material end, we have as many senses as we have cells and corpuscles in our bodies. Viewing it from the spiritual side, the really substantial side of life, we have only one sense, which is God himself, the sense or soul of all creation; and this one sense builds uncounted millions of Marconi stations by which it gains intelligence, sensations, from all space.

And still life is building better, more sensitive marconigraphs. There are those in whom a sixth sense is well developed, and a seventh hinted at. And the scientist points to great gaps of vibrations not yet touched by man, not to mention the ultra-violet vibrations not yet imagined. Man is destined to explore them all.

The sixth sense of clairvoyance and clairaudience corresponds with the sixth principle of transmutation. The seventh sense, intuition, clear-knowing, corresponds to the seventh principle of sensation or blessing, and it results in the so-called cosmic consciousness.

All these principles and senses are inherent in every human being, and in every atom and corpuscle of creation. In due time every individual will come under dominance of each and every principle; but always the entire seven are working subconsciously in you, if not consciously. And always the entire seven are present and active, consciously or unconsciously, in every life cell of creation.

Nothing has been left out of anybody's make-up; everything is in its place, awaiting its turn in your consciousness.

5

THE NEW THOUGHT PLATFORM.

THIS brings us to the statement of our Twelve Planks of the New Thought Platform, as a basis for future instruction in the development of the individual—for the joy of all.

Here is our platform, broad enough, strong enough for not only the "hundred and forty and four thousand" elect, but for all mankind, and womankind, and even for all the ITS of creation:—

1. God is all-present Mind, whose mode of motion is thought.

2. Man is God's Idea; men are trains of thought in God's mind; "man is a statement of beliefs."

3. Thought on its active side is Will or Desire; on its negative side it is Wisdom.

4. Desire and Wisdom inhere in God and in all his thoughts and in man and in man's thoughts. Desire and Wisdom hold planets in their orbits and project comets on their course. They likewise hold man in his place and urge him to work out the God-idea within him by building more and more stately mansions in mind, and in materials. Desire and Wisdom control man's thoughts, too. Not even one "idle word," or idle thought, is too slight to be swayed by the desire within it, and by desires outside of it which are akin.

5. Desire is the primal force of Attraction inherent in every atom and in every organization of atoms through all creation.

6. Wisdom is the Pattern, the Idea, inherent in God, and every atom, and in every organization of atoms in all creation.

7. Desire and Wisdom constitute also the free ethers (or God) in which all creation moves and has its being, and by inspiring which it lives and grows.

8. Life is a Great School in which we learn wisdom by doing things.

9. All ways of doing things—or people—are open to us, wise and unwise. We may use either or both ways. We find by experience that the "way of the transgressor is hard," while "wisdom's ways are ways of pleasantness and all her paths are peace."

By experience we prove wisdom's ways are what we desire— are not wisdom and desire One from eternity to eternity?

Transgressor of what ? Of the law of all being, the Law of Oneness, Wisdom, and Desire. (How would you act toward another if you could see your Oneness with him and realize your wisdom and love?) 10. Man's desire is inseparable from his wisdom—he desires what he thinks is for his good.

He is also one with the universal sea of wisdom and desire which lies just above his consciousness. This universal wisdom desires for and through him, and often overrules for his good the good he thought he desired. At the time it seems hard that he cannot have the thing he desired; later he sees that it was because he was not, in his consciousness, wise enough to desire the right thing in the right place.

This One Universal Consciousness is ever urging every man to right action, before the man has wisdom enough to recognize what the right action should be.

This spirit of wisdom lightens every man that comes into the world, and continues to press for expression through him, every moment as long as he lives. The more complete a man's dependence upon this universal spirit that speaks within, the surer he is to choose always the path of wisdom, peace, and pleasantness.

The world is growing in knowledge— the only way a mental world can grow. Man's mistakes come through dependence upon his present fund of wisdom and knowledge, considering himself apart from other humans, and separate from God, the Universal Spirit of all wisdom.

11. The things that are unseen are the true forces and substances of life— Wisdom, Love or Desire, Ideals. The things that are seen are ever changing for something better.

Therefore, we look within for our peace and happiness and we value a clear conscience above rubies. We value above loves, lands, and honors that inner quiet, the well-done of the Universal Spirit witnessing with ours, that all is well no matter what passes.

12. But it is not all resignation. Next comes creation. Being mental creatures we think new things into being.

Do we desire a thing? Then it is ours by right, provided we can have it without robbing another. The next thing is to desire it steadily and think it into being.

Health, Wealth, Wisdom, Love, Success, all may be ours; not only without robbing another; they may enrich others through being ours. But we must think them into being without thinking anything away from others. The means by which we go to work to earn money must be blest by those who buy as well as those who sell. We desire for others all we desire for ourselves, plus all they may desire for themselves.

The chief end of man is to glorify good and enjoy working it out forever.

6

EVOLUTION AND THE ABSOLUTE, AND PERPETUAL LIFE.

EARLY all new thought people believe in evolution, along with all orthodox scientists of the day. But here and there you will find a teacher of some cult that declares positively there is no such thing as evolution ; that it is a myth, a mirage, maya, illusion; that there is only the Absolute and everything else is poppycock and tommy-rot, or words to that effect.

We receive hundreds of letters from beginners bewildered by these conflicting teachings. "Which is right?" they beg to know.

They are both right in a sense; and they are both wrong in a sense.

"The things which are not seen are eternal; the things which are seen are temporal,"—temporary, forever changing,—said Paul. But the absolutist new thoughter jumps a long way and arrives at the conclusion that the things which are not seen are eternal, absolute, while the things that are seen are useless, chaotic nothings to be ignored, despised, denied, and lived above.

The Christian Science branch of new thought attributes all matter to "carnal mind," and carnal mind it identifies as the devil. Material things are not under the law of God, they assert, neither can be, therefore matter and all material things are evil, the devil, and we must despise them and live outside of them. They, too, are right, in a sense.

God is the Absolute, unchanging, eternal in the heavens; the same yesterday, to-day, and forever; the omniscient, omnipotent, omnipresent One; the only actor in all action; the only thinker behind all thought; the one life and energy that fills all space and time; the One found alike in heaven and in hell; God the First Cause, the One Creator; God the Absolute and intangible I AM IT who inhabits space eternally.

Here is your absolute, of whom the absolutist prates. God is absolute, changeless. But his THOUGHTS are ever changing within him; his thought-built universe evolutes from the beginning. And beginning itself is eternal. Every blade of grass that grows, every tree, every insect, bird, animal, is an orderly evolution of thought within the Absolute; and every child that comes into the world repeats each step of evolution from "the beginning" described in Genesis, up to the present time. In the womb he passes subconsciously through every phase of evolution from the first forming of a sphere out of the fiery mist, up through every vegetable and animal plane to the plane of completed man; and he comes forth "an acme of things accomplished" by God's thought plus man's up to the present time, and "an encloser of things to be" accomplished by God and man in all millenniums to come.

There Is this active thought side of God, and creation is IT— including you and me. God thinks; and he does not think the absolute and unchangeable any more than you do, or the absolutist teacher does.

God the absolute is not content with Nirvana, the state of changeless bliss feeling. If he had been, you and I and creation had never been. God feels Nirvana at the center of him, as you and I may feel it (of which more anon), but he is not content with that; he wants to think out bliss to the very circumference of him; he wants to prove himself in ideas, to think out thought-creatures who will "enjoy him forever," enjoy with him forever.

So God BEGAN to think. His spirit moved on the face of the Nirvana deep and his nebulous feeling began to precipitate in thought forms of whirling corpuscles and worlds; the "morning stars sang together" with him. This was the beginning of things, the beginning of evolution, the beginning of God's thinking that resulted at last in man, who could think with him as well as within him and by his power.

"The father worketh hitherto (to the point of evolving me)," said Jesus, "and now I work." "I in the Father, and he in me, and we in YOU," Jesus explained. The evolution of man is the involution of God; evolution is the concentration of God's life, nature, character, into countless millions of images and likenesses of himself. Men are the facets of God; each focuses all the colors of his spectrum. To this end God thought and thinks: that man find himself "an infinite little copy of God," ready to carry thinking still further.

So God "gave man dominion" over all things he had thought out up to and including man himself. And with God conscious man came the end of new orders of creation—after that comes nature plus "art"—plus man's thought and man's work.

Don't you see that God was lonesome, and set to work to think out (thought being his only mode of activity) a lot of self-thinking, self-willing people to enjoy living and thinking and loving with him?

I doubt God's knowing in the beginning just how to do this. He had to experiment. All along the way of evolution lie the bones of creatures God thought out and then abandoned for higher forms. These fossil creatures are still preserved to us, that we may see the mistakes God made before he succeeded in thinking out a satisfactory pattern of a man.

But at last he got him made, pronounced him good, turned over the remainder of the job to him, and rested from his lonely and hitherto unappreciated labors.

And then man took up the work of evolution. As the Father had life and will, love, wisdom in himself, so had he given to the son to have life, will, wisdom, love, thinking power in himself. Then God drove him out of the Garden of Eden to work out the dominion given him; dominion over every beast of the field and every beast of his own breast; dominion over earth, fire, water, and air within and without.

And man has evoluted things apace. It is a far cry from the first fig-leaf apron to the dressmakers' convention held in New York every spring, and to the ready-to-wear clothing a man buys on sight; from flint-and-tinder fires to Lucifer matches and Gurney heaters; from cave dwellings to twentieth century mansions and hotels; from wooden sticks to Oliver plows; from pine knots to electric lighting; from the spring at the roadside to the springs piped into your kitchen; from the pony express to the twentieth century limited, the telegraph, telephone, and wireless; from the log and paddle of Ab to the Mauretania and the Wright brothers; from the stone ax and spearhead to United Steel and our navy's tour of the world; from the jungle of Eden to a New York of skyscrapers; from hieroglyphs on stone to the Congressional library and Carnegie; from Adam to Christ, and to Roosevelt, Paderewski, Rockefeller.

It takes man to help God put on the finishing touches. That's what God made man for—to help him think still farther and better, and to enjoy doing it forever; to make a paradise out of this earth and then conquer the stars. If you are critical you can find lots of mistakes man has made in trying to improve the earth; but he is abandoning his mistakes as fast as he can, just as God abandoned reptilian monstrosities as soon as he thought beyond them.

And every day we are evolving better ideas and putting them to use. Every day we are getting better command of ourselves, our wills; every day we are doing better work; every day we are coming nearer together, working more for the good of all than for the good of self.

Surely we are "growing in wisdom and in knowledge"—the only way there is for mental creatures to grow. Man and God are now working together to create "whatsoever things they desire." Between them they are daily discovering new and greater things to desire, and daily they are working together to think out and work out those things into being.

God being omnipotence, omniscience, omnipresence, and God being the backer of man, do you think there is any desirable thing that they cannot bring into being? Don't you see that with such a backing any man's desire is but the prophecy of its own fulfillment?

What if desire is exactly identical with Newton's force of gravitation? What if desire draws the thing desired? Haven't you noticed in your own life a hundred, a thousand little cases wherein a desired thing came to you in the nick of time? I have.

Ponder this: When the desired thing does not come to you or to me, and come readily, it is because something in you inhibits the action of desire, just as you inhibit the action of gravitation this minute by holding this book from being drawn to the ground.

Desire and gravitation are identical, the very same force. The earth desires and attracts this book; you desire and hold the book away from the earth.

How can you do this, when earth is so much larger? You do it by concentration of desire, not by bulk of desiring atoms. You are an involution of all creation, with power over all creation. You overcome all forces below you and by this exercise you develop energy for still greater overcomings.

Whatsoever thing you desire will come to you just as soon as you can find and remove the inhibiting desire. For desire, gravitation, attraction is inhibited by greater desire, gravitation, attraction.

Sometimes another's desire is set upon a thing you desire and his attraction inhibits yours.

But in ninety-nine out of one hundred times it is some counter desire within you that keeps you from receiving what you desire; or it is the insulating of your desire-power by fear.

In any event it is merely a matter of time, patience, and desire-persistence, when you will be able to get around or over that inhibiting desire.

There is absolutely no true ideal in the imagination of any man but it will be desire-drawn into expression sooner or later. The millennium that has been desired in all ages is surely being drawn into being.

And here comes in the overcoming of death—the last enemy that shall be ousted by man. The prophets will surely be justified; death will give place to life incorruptible, right here on this earth. Even the material scientists are seeing it now; are seeing what the religionist has always known by intuition.

About death and its overcoming we hear conflicting teaching, too, as about evolution and the absolute. "There is no death," says one; "we are eternal now." "Death is the last enemy that shall be overcome," says his opponent. Both are right. In the absolute is no death, no beginning, and no end. On the unseen side—at the center of the star—we are all one life, deathless, immortal. Men have felt this always. But on the seen side of life, the thought-built side, we certainly do die, as well as live. Death is doubtless a door into a new room of life, but nevertheless it is death. And it is this very death of the thought-built body as a whole that the prophets declared should be overcome as the last enemy.

Somatic death is necessary to expedite the evolution of man. Man is a growing child, and it is easier to slough off an outgrown body and begin over than to spend time and energy making over the body to fit the growing-up individual.

But it is only a matter of getting rid of mistakes. When we learn to slough off our mistakes daily, hourly, as a little child does, we shall keep soft, elastic, clean bodies that can do their dying daily, instead of all in a bunch.

The outgrowing of death in the body is a matter of desire. Nobody likes death—everybody would be glad to abolish it. Man's desire would have found the way long ago except for one thing:

Each individual has lived so strenuously trying to subdue his environment and earn a living that he has TIRED of living and literally lost his desire-grip on life.

Not until man gets earth conditions made over into pretty much of a paradise can he faithfully desire to stay here without change. Death of the body is so wrapped up with economic conditions that the two will have to be overcome together.

To so live as not to become tired of living is the key to overcoming death of the body.

And how could one enjoy living eternally with the spur of poverty nipping him, or the sight of poverty-nipped neighbors forever before him? First must Edward Bellamy's dream come true; and thousands still will die in working it out.

After that everlasting life in the flesh will come easy. And along with it will come levitation, rapid transit to and from other worlds.

7

COSMIC CONSCIOUSNESS.

MAN is mind, one with the Great Mind. And in this mind is his thought-built body. Instead of your being a mind or soul in a body, you are mind with a thought-built body inside of it! You are not a mind, but MIND, universal mind, God mind. At the center of you, which is also the circumference, you are God. "One with the Father," as Jesus said.

The seers of all the ages have known this. Listen to these "Last Lines," by Emily Bronte:— *"No coward soul is mine, No trembler in the world's storm-troubled sphere: I see Heaven's glories shine, And faith shines equal, arming me from fear.*

"O God within my breast, Almighty, ever-present Deity! Life— that in me has rest, As I—undying Life—have power in thee! "Vain are the thousand creeds

That move men's hearts: unutterably vain; Worthless as withered weeds, Or idlest froth amid the boundless main, "To waken doubt in one Holding so fast by thine infinity; So surely anchored on The steadfast rock of immortality. "With wide-embracing love Thy spirit animates eternal years, Pervades and broods above, Changes, sustains, dissolves, creates, and rears. "Though earth and man were gone, And suns and universes ceased to be, And Thou wert left alone, Every existence would exist in Thee. "There is no room for Death, Nor atom that his might could render void; Thou—THOU art Being and Breath, And what THOU art may never be destroyed." And there is that beautiful little poem, "Illusion," by our own American poet, Ella Wheeler Wilcox:—

God and I in space alone, And nobody else in view. And "Where are the people, O Lord," I said, "The earth below and the sky o'erhead, And the dead whom once I knew?" "That was a dream," God smiled and said; "A dream that seemed to be true; There were no people living or dead, There was no earth and no sky o'erhead— There was only Myself and you." "Why do I feel no fear," I asked, "Meeting YOU here this way? For I have sinned, I know full well; And is there heaven, and is there hell, And is this the Judgment Day?"

"Nay! those were but dreams," the great God said, "Dreams that have ceased to be; There is no such thing as fear, or sin; There is no you—you never have been— There is nothing at all .but Me!" Kate Boehme illustrates this as well as it can be illustrated to a three-dimension intellect with a star.

The points of the star represent the individual's consciousness, the visible person. Trace these points back toward the center and you find all are one.

Imagine the universe as a great star, each individual as a point of the star. The more completely one lives in the consciousness of his material self the farther he gets away from consciousness of the center where all are one.

But it is quite possible to extend one's consciousness until it takes in the spiritual center as well as the material circumference of life.

It is possible to go still farther and come into sympathy, into consciousness with other points of the great star. I have dwelt much upon the oneness of all beings because it is the very most important plank in the whole new thought platform, and without it there is no basis for correct reasoning, or for right understanding and judgment. To reason and judge by that which we see at the point of the star is to misjudge life and people and go ever astray in our reckonings. The points of the star head every which way, and on the very tip of each sits Gradgrind, with insanity and death straight before him!

On the other hand, to get clear away from the point of the star, to live too much in the consciousness of unmaterial life, is to invite disintegration and death of the individual.

I have sometimes wondered if Emerson's softening of the brain was not due in a measure, at least, to this very thing; if he did not dwell so much with the absolute, with the oversoul, valuing so little the forms and facts of material life, that the channels which thought must run in grew shallow and soft. And it is a fact that nearly every devoted spiritualist one meets is anything but positively healthy and wealthy on the material plane.

"Judge not according to outward appearances," said Jesus, "but judge right judgment." Right judgment comes from getting a fair view of all the premises. Right judgment begins at the center, the point of oneness of motive, and reasons outward; while unright judgment begins at the point of the star and stays there.

The only safe way is to stand on the solid earth, value the world of created things as proof of the center of life and power, look to the center for power and wisdom, but be not content until you have used the power and wisdom to change material things.

A man is a point of the universal star, and his center is the center of every other star point.

To judge another by yourself is scientific; but first be sure you know yourself—from circumference to center and back again.

NOW: God is the Universal Presence of Will and Wisdom, who dreamed a universe and then proceeded to think it out.

Robert Fulton was a point of this Universal Presence of will and wisdom, made in its image and of its very substance, breathing momently its essence, its dream, its will and wisdom.

Robert Fulton dreamed a steamboat, and then proceeded to think it out. Others, too, caught the dream—caught more of it than Fulton could—and then proceeded to think it out. The Mauretania is the result, the expression of that dream up to date; and still the dream is growing; still the "pattern" is coming down from the heavens, from the One Presence, to be caught by man and thought out into form.

And many were the mistakes made in thinking out the steamboat dream up to date, and every mistake was a teacher. As fast as man learned from a mistake he corrected it and passed on.

So even the mistakes were good, when considered in regard to the man, the dream, and its working out. For man, being all mental, grows only by learning ; and mistakes teach him, as well as successes. Therefore are mistakes good. You realize this when you really understand what man is and how he grows by catching on to and working out his point of the great star-dream of the Whole.

His individual dream is his set of specifications from the great Architect Dreamer of space and eternity; and his wage for thinking out these specifications into being is joy ever growing, and houses, lands, gratitude, fame, and personal loves added.

To be right with one's part of the great dream is to make a magnet of one's self that draws every desirable thing. To do the will of the Father as seen in your dream or ideal is the necessary thing.

When Theodore Roosevelt was new on his presidency job some of his party leaders thought he needed instruction. Said one of them, "Mr. Roosevelt, you must continually feel for the pulse of the people and be governed by that." "Why should I spend time feeling for the people's pulse," demanded Roosevelt, "when every honest man knows in his own heart what is right?"

It is by feeling the universal pulse beat in his own heart and acting upon it that Roosevelt is doing so much for the world. "I am just an average man," said he in an interview; "the only difference between me and any ordinary man is that when I see a thing ought to be done I go straight and do it."

Other men as brilliant and as good get tangled in personal considerations, bad habits of living, red tape. Roosevelt keeps his eye on his dream, his specifications from the heaven within, and puts in his best lick wherever and whenever there is a chance. If anybody gets in the way of that lick so much the worse for him.

McKinley put in his best licks after first seeing that all his friends were safe out of the way, and all the proprieties observed. He knew as well as Roosevelt or Lincoln what was right, but he couldn't do it if it hurt the feelings of his friends—or his wife.

Did you ever read Kipling's "How the Ship Found Herself"? If not, do so. It presents to the imagination a perfect picture of the way the universe is finding itself. Kipling describes the new ship, every mast, sail, and bit of timber, every bolt and screw in place, each well fitted, polished, complacent, and proud in its proper place.

Then the ship is launched and sails away to sea. As the ship plows ahead, rising to the crest of a great wave only to plunge headlong into the trough, all the little screws and bolts, as well as masts and sails, begin to creak and squeak and shriek complaints. "Oh, you are grinding me to pieces!" shrieks the bolt against the wood. The mast snaps at the deck; the stanchions groan that they are being ruined and can't hold on much longer; the yards and masts shriek that their backs are breaking and the sails ought to be slit to ribbons for abusing them so. Every individual scrap of metal that goes to make up the great ship has its own complaint to make about the way its neighbor abuses it.

And all this time the ship keeps steadily on, the sailors polish the decks and keep the brasses bright, loose a screw here, tighten a bolt there, drop a bit of oil where it is needed. And after a while the various parts get used to their places and their work, the creaks and shrieks and groans grow softer, and finally everything settles contentedly to its work, and the sharp complaints die away to a full-toned murmur of understanding and good will toward each other and their work. And so the good ship finds herself.

The world is like that. All these ages we have been crying against our neighbors and our work. We have misunderstood and undervalued ourselves and each other. But always the good ship has kept steadily on her course, and we have been oiled and polished, tightened up or loosened out as need arose, but ever we have been kept to our place in spite of misunderstanding and complaint—unless we happened to be the flea, or rat, or stowaway variety that sometimes infests a ship!

And now, in this nineteenth and twentieth centuries, we common parts of the ship are finding ourselves as part of the whole.

8

HOW TO BECOME COSMO-CONSCIOUS.

THE consciousness of self in relation to the whole universe and God is called cosmic consciousness—the consciousness of the cosmos.

It is truly a state of consciousness only and it results from an attitude of mind that some people are born with and others achieve by deliberate practice.

It is, too, a matter of growth; for no man can achieve cosmic consciousness until he has grown up mentally to a certain height.

It is like the growth of a seed in the ground. A grain of corn comes to itself in the earth. Its individual consciousness is born down under the sod. The warmth of the sun draws it upward; by answering the sun's urge it sends out roots, finds its food, and does its work. Probably it complains and strains, even as you and I. And ever it aspires, even as we; ever it stretches upward in answer to the sun's call, even as you and I aspire toward the spiritual sun that beams unseen for us, hidden by the denseness of our earth surroundings.

And so the little grain of corn does its work and frets its little heart and ever reaches upward, until at last it pokes its little head above the earth and for the first time gets a glimpse of something besides itself. Under the sod the grain of corn was supremely conscious of itself and its limitations and strivings; now it sees other people, the earth and its relation to the whole; it has come into something that to it is a sort of cosmic consciousness.

The coming forth of the butterfly from the chrysalis is another parallel to this cosmic-consciousness experience; also the coming forth of the child from the womb. In each case it is a matter of coming forth from a cocoon of self-consciousness into a consciousness of life, of other people and one's relations to them.

The ordinary philosophy of life held by the common run of people to-day is a mental cocoon of self-consciousness in which he grows, wriggling, twisting, and complaining more or less, until he grows up to the point of bursting that self-philosophy and coming out of his shell into consciousness of a world in which he is only one of many all urged by a common life purpose from one God. To really sense this, as well as to see it intellectually, is to experience real cosmic consciousness.

This birth into the cosmic sense generally comes as suddenly and completely as the birth of a butterfly or a babe. There is no going back again into the chrysalis, no going back into the old little-self life.

But one catches intellectual glimpses of the cosmic before he is really born into the cosmic consciousness, just as the grub may catch glimpses of the world through his shell, may feel his growing wings though they are not yet unfolded; just as the chick may peep at the world before he fully emerges from the shell.

The Bible states that they that come unto God "must believe that he is, and that he is a rewarder of them that diligently seek him." Even so, those who come into the cosmic sense must believe that they are one with the cosmos, so that they desire or aspire to know the cosmos better and to feel with it.

In due time comes the experience of cosmic consciousness, which is an experience, but not a provable thing. It is a religious experience, known by the one who experiences it, but utterly intangible to one who is not ready to emerge from the grub state. As well talk color to one born blind as to talk cosmic consciousness to the ordinary man.

Or, rather, to the back-number man; for it is the ordinary men and women of the twentieth century who are now coming into the world of cosmic consciousness.

The religious experience commonly called conversion may be likened to the state of the grub when he first feels his embryo wings and catches a glimpse of the world through his shriveling shell. He is still held fast in his cramped environment, but he begins to realize that there is something larger that he will find in time.

This is where the idea of heaven after death came in; the human grub of past generations died in the grub state; he never came to the open of cosmic consciousness, so his heaven did come after death, as his instinct and theology taught him. The masses died thus. Only here and there a seer or a Christ found the cosmic consciousness of heaven within and now.

And these, too, realized that the grub man needed time and countless reincarnations before he could find heaven within and now. This accounts for so much future tense in the Bible, and harmonizes it with the present tense of Jesus' teaching about heaven and oneness.

The religious experience called by old-fashioned Methodists "sanctification" is nothing more or less than the cosmic consciousness. Many sought sanctification but few found it— though more than a few claimed it.

Conversion means turning to God, the Cosmic One, and trying to imitate Jesus; but sanctification means giving to God yourself, all you know and all you don't know, and finding yourself in him and him in you as your very heart, desire, and moving impulse.

One sees either of these experiences intellectually first—"as through a glass darkly"; as through the thinning cocoon—and, seeing, desires it. Then he meets the conditions and experiences it "in his heart" or emotional center, which is the center of the star, you know, where God is.

This "heart" of you is what modern psychologists call the subconscious or subliminal mind, of which more anon. Suffice it here to say that the subconscious mind is about 95 per cent, of you, and that it is like a deep reservoir filled with thoughts and concepts sent into it by way of your conscious intellect.

The conscious mind is a mere surface or gateway to this big reservoir of you. Not until the 95 per cent, reservoir of your subconscious mind has accepted a truth can you really embody that truth and be saved by it. This is why the old-fashioned religionist belittled intellect; he knew it counted for naught as long as "the heart" was wrong.

A hundred years ago it was fashionable to seek conversion, because the time was ripe for a great many people to come into that consciousness. In this day and age many of the sons and daughters and grandsons and granddaughters of those converted a hundred years ago are born and brought up already converted; they are born with a degree of spiritual consciousness never dreamed of before this age, except by the occasional prophet and savior.

I knew in Oregon two old people nearing the threescore-and-ten milepost, who were born in this consciousness. I quizzed them long and often about it. It was a marvel to me then; now it is beautifully clear. They were born converted, and in early youth they came into sanctification, or cosmic consciousness. Their beautiful faces and lovely lives manifested it.

My mother was converted when she was about thirty-four, and died two years later, when I was nine. I thought of spiritual things when very young, and was converted when I was less than twenty-five. My two children have practically grown up in spiritual thought, and I am looking for their children to be born converted.

When I was about twenty-seven I came into the experience called then sanctification, now named cosmic consciousness. So by the law of evolution my grandchildren or great-grandchildren may be born cosmic-sensitive! In Dr. Maurice Bucke's book on "Cosmic Consciousness" he gives the following as the truths which the new consciousness revealed to him:—

1. He "came to see and know that the cosmos is not dead matter but a living presence."

2. "That the soul of man is immortal; that the universe is so built and ordered that without any peradventure all things work together for the good of each and all."

3. "That the foundation principle of the world is what we call love, and that the happiness of every one is in the long run absolutely certain."

To convince your subconscious self of these three truths is to achieve the cosmic sense; for whatever that subconscious self really accepts is what you feel to be true. The intellectual concept does not save you. How can it, when conscious mind is but five per cent, of your total consciousness? You must be convinced of a truth before you are saved by that truth. A line from Shakespeare points the way: "Assume a virtue if you have it not."

To affirm a truth, acting upon it as well as you can, ends in subconscious conviction and knowing, or "feeling" that truth. Why not, since we are mental beings?

A high truth firmly held will make over the entire mind, conscious and subconscious. To say the truth over to yourself is to "speak the Word" that creates and re-creates you. Without the Word, the affirmation, the mental statement, is not anything made or remade in you.

To achieve the cosmic consciousness, affirm it, affirm it. Take special seasons every day, preferably the first minutes after waking and the last before going to sleep, for special realization practice. First, breathe fully and relax every muscle. Then affirm positively to yourself that the universe is a living and loving presence and that all things work together for the good and joy of each and all. Affirm this several times, positively.

Then relax as fully as possible—get limp all over—and imagine that One Living Presence of Love enfolding you warmly, filling you with the love and wisdom of Itself. Think how you would feel if you could feel this to be true.

Then go about your work and never mind the affirmations or the cosmic consciousness, either, for that matter. If you are faithful to this realization practice you will soon find yourself remembering it and thinking and acting from it without trying to.

And eventually you will find not only your thoughts but your very instinct acting upon the statements you have made for yourself.

The more good will, enthusiasm, and imagination you can put into this practice the sooner the real cosmic consciousness will be yours. It will be yours eventually, anyway, but you can hasten it by every bit of aspiration, affirmation, imagination, and steady enthusiasm you put into it.

9

TELEPATHY: A NEW VIEW.

MAN is "an infinite little copy of God"; and everything in this world is a copy of some portion of man. Every invention existed first in man's mind. Man has a complete photographing outfit within him—camera, lens, negative, dark room, developers, art gallery, and all. The telegraph and telephone came from within man.

You cannot name an invention of any sort from the tiniest and simplest to the greatest and most complex; you cannot name a form in nature, nor a principle of growth in nature, that has not its parallel and original in man. And more inventions are coming every day —all coming out of man.

And by these things that come out of man we are learning what is in man. One of the most significant things that has come out of man so far is the Marconi system of wireless telegraph. We haven't got the wireless telegraph all out of man yet—many improvements have been made since wireless telegraphy was first announced, and more are coming.

But enough of it has been evolved to give us a very good idea of how men communicate without using either of the ordinary five senses.

Telepathy is the word coined to cover a lot of cases of communication not explainable through the five senses.

Such as that case of Bishop Taylor. He was traveling his circuit one night, and a spring freshet carried coach and horses off their footing, the bishop barely escaping with his life. His wife and daughter were sleeping in their separate rooms at home, a hundred miles away. At the exact hour of the bishop's accident wife and daughter were roused by a terrible fear, and both cried out that the bishop's life was in danger. Later they quieted down and slept again. Two days later the bishop recounted his experience to them, saying that at the moment of the accident he gave himself up for lost, and his soul went out to his wife and daughter in heart-breaking farewell.

I need not recount other tales of the sort—nearly everybody has had similar experiences of his own, or knows someone who has. That, under certain conditions, men do communicate with each other without using any of the ordinary known means for such purpose is a fact too well established now to elicit discussion.

But the method of such communication is an open question the whole civilized world is engaged in discussing. Several societies for psychical research spend much time in sifting evidence with a view to settling upon someone theory as official. They are after a sort of Newtonian law that cannot be disputed.

So far the results are a mass of evidence, more or less reliable, and several conflicting theories. The Spiritualists say spirits do it all. Professor Hyslop is now convinced that spirits do some of the communicating. Others throw spirits to the dogs and insist that every spirit in the flesh is able to send and to receive mental messages—under certain unknown conditions.

Now please remember that all these views are merely individual opinions, based upon the same mass of circumstantial evidence. Nobody has proved anything beyond the phenomena themselves. And all these people are now inclined to agree that probably every man has within himself the ability to telepath, and that probably most of the common experiences of telepathy take place without the intervention of other spirits, in the body or out.

I am inclined to think that all these phenomena take place within and by the power of the individual himself, without outside disembodied spirits having anything whatever to do with it. I believe man is his own telegraph and marconigraph for sending and receiving messages, and that the higher his mind projects into the ethers of pure spirit, the cosmic sense, the more he will learn about his own marconigraph and the better he will be able to use it.

This does not mean that I don't believe in disembodied spirits, or in their power to communicate with man. There may be disembodied conscious souls; I neither believe in them nor disbelieve in them. The case stands simply "not proven." The phenomena that convinced Professor Hyslop did not come up to my "test conditions." It seemed to me that he accepted spirits on the say-so of a woman who afterward discredited her own testimony. Whereupon Professor Hyslop discredited her to save his scientific face! Of course the professor is a trained observer; so am I. And I have nothing to lose and the truth to gain if new evidence changes my mind.

But of this I am reasonably sure: that if there are disembodied conscious spirits who communicate with men they are equipped with something like the same sort of telepath apparatus that embodied spirits have.

Now let us see what we can discover from the wireless telegraph of Marconi, for verily man is like unto it, as Jesus might say. Analogy is after all the best proof of a thing, particularly when the subject of the analogy comes out of man with whom the comparison is made.

First, then, the wireless telegraph is based upon the ethers in which we live and move and have our being. The heavenly ethers convey its every message. It is the heavenly ethers through which the message is conveyed, and it is the earth which receives the current. Up in the heavens, at the top of a tall rod, the message is received, and down the rod it comes, to be received close to earth if not in the very earth itself.

Think of space as a living, love-vibrating presence; a divine presence that vibrates perhaps to the tone of Nirvana. Every activity of man and of whirling world interrupts the current of this basic Nirvana vibration, and thereby conveys its import to other individuals and to God.

In speaking I send out certain sounds that interrupt the etheric current in certain definite rhythm. Your ears are fine instruments for measuring the current-interruptions I am making in the ethers. Seeing, hearing, smelling, tasting, feeling, are all based upon this same interruption of the basic vibration-tone of the universal substance, which is electric in its nature.

The telephone, telegraph, and wireless all are based upon this same principle of conveying messages by interruption of an electric current. In telegraphing, the electricity is made to vibrate through the wire, and the interruptions are made by tapping a key. In wireless telegraphing the vibration of the upper air is used, the interruptions coming from the key. Close to earth there are so many other interruptions of current taking place that the wireless key cannot make itself distinguished.

Note the difference between telegraph and wireless: in telegraphing, the current is confined to the wire and the message follows that line only; but a wireless message goes out in all directions, as the rays of the sun go out.

To get a wire you must be on the line. To get a wireless you can be anywhere; the only necessity is that you are keyed to the message sent. Unless a ship's instrument is keyed aright it cannot receive the most insistent message sent out from a wireless station.

To have a line up to the clear spaces, and to be tuned to the sender, are the two absolute requirements of wireless telegraphy.

And of telepathy. The man whose thought stays close to earth; who lives in the tangle of cross-purposes; who looks on the outward appearances as the important thing; such a man must depend upon his five earth-senses for most of the messages he receives. But the man who runs up a line into the clear blue of the cosmic senses receives telepaths and spiritual "leads" the earthy man never dreams of. I wonder if intuition is the heaven-wire by which we receive our wireless messages. And I am sure aspiration and inspiration are messages sent over the heaven-wire.

In connection with this idea I recall certain discoveries of Dr. Baraduc's in Paris, and several alleged photograph reproductions of strange psychic phenomena produced by him. Dr. Baraduc has succeeded in photographing what he calls the mental ball. This, he says, is a luminous sphere that floats at the end of a misty cable three or four feet above the head of a person. Dr. Baraduc thinks it is through this misty cable and mental ball that people receive telepathic messages. It may be true. If so I wonder if the wireless telegraph people could not solve some of their difficulties by putting a metal globe at the top of their poles.

Dr. Baraduc says that at death this mental ball and its anchoring cable float free and dissolve like smoke. He shows photos of this phenomenon. He likewise shows photos of the spirit or life or aura floating off from the body and dissolving in long vapor-like filaments and streamers.

I cannot prove to the five-senses man that he has within him the spiritual instruments for sending and receiving messages by wireless. None of these spiritual things can be proved to such a man, any more than color can be proved to one born blind to it. Spiritual things are discerned by new spiritual senses. "Ye must be born again," if you are still densely material.

If you cannot see by analogy, your spiritual, cosmic-sense eyes are indeed closed, and more time must be allowed before you come out of the grub-state.

Let us assume telepathy and learn how to use it. Nothing like doing a thing to teach us the truth about it. It may be that telepathy has not always been a practical thing among all human beings; that it was merely inherent, as the butterfly's wings were inherent in the grub; waiting for a certain stage of development to unfold it.

All through the ages there have been a few peculiar persons who manifested the ability to telepath. And many people of the psychic order have had special experiences in thought transference. But all cases seem to have been sporadic and impossible to repeat. Never until this age has there been any attempt made to classify telepathic phenomena and utilize the law of them. All this thinking about it means that the hour is at hand for unfolding our telepathic wings, so to speak.

One of the first requisites for telepathic communication seems to be that mysterious something called "rapport." Two people who love each other and are harmonious in thought can exchange thoughts without tangible means of conveyance, while two inharmonious persons seem to make no exchange at all.

Dr. Baraduc and his late wife communicated telepathically, and Dr. Baraduc believes and seems to have proved by his photographic experiments that there was a sort of spiritual cord between him and his wife, communicating through those mental balls of which I spoke before. Many seers have declared that they could see filmy cords connecting certain people together.

Such spiritual lines probably do exist between certain people. It would not be strange if these very spiritual lines were "the pattern in the heavens" that inspired the telegraph; and that one's thoughts are the "Morse code" understood and translated by those on the line.

It looks, then, as if there is a telepathy of wires as well as a telepathy of wireless. And the former is more easily proved and attracts more attention than the latter, because it is more nearly developed as a provable thing.

And it looks as if language is truly inspired, as the psalmist says; since certain people are really "attached to each other," as we say,—attached by spiritual lines that are real telepath wires. And this reminds me of another phase of telegraphy and telepathy: we are to have color pictures flashed over the wires, just as many people have had visions flashed over their telepathic wires. If one admits this hint at a hypothesis, it is easy to see how to cultivate telepathy. Cultivate harmony and love and community of interests.

Telepathy by wire has existed for nobody can guess how long. I have seen many cases of it, where two people exchanged thoughts many times every day often without even guessing that they did so. William's mother and I must have a line up, judging by the number of messages we exchange on little items concerning the household. And William and I are always exchanging thoughts, sometimes sending and receiving messages by intention, but more often involuntarily. We have no mental reservations between us to act as grounders for our thoughts.

And this brings me to the main reason that almost settles me in the belief that telepathy by spiritual wire, and telepathy by wireless, are being unfolded in our consciousness just as telegraph and wireless are being unfolded in the world.

I said William and I have no mental reservations to ground our messages. Absolute honesty is the electricity that charges the spiritual wires between people and makes possible the transference of thought. A steady current of good will is the energy that carries the thought. Disingenuousness insulates one's mind so that no spiritual current of good will goes out to another. The deceitful, secretive person keeps his good will for himself.

Do you see what a wise provision of nature, or life, or God, this is? Suppose all the villains of all the ages had been able to run out lines to their victims and read their thoughts, purposes, and plans. Suppose the village gossip could thus get a line on everything.

As long as there are villains there must be means of insulating thought, and nature has provided that the villain himself afford that means. He puts up walls of secrecy and dwells within in fear of what is outside. His good will to himself turns sour and ferments, breeding all sorts of boogers to scare him. So, "the wicked flee when no man pursueth."

Not until a man catches glimpses of his oneness with all creatures is it safe to trust him to read the thoughts of others. Just in proportion as his good will flows outward will he come into rapport with others, where he can sometimes read their thoughts.

Selfishness and its secretiveness and fear are the barriers against rapports with those about us. When we are evolved enough to throw down these barriers, be absolutely honorable and honest and kind with our neighbors and ourselves, we shall find rapports establishing on all sides.

To think and do and good-will unto others as you would have them think and do and good-will unto you, is the first and indispensable condition for telepathy: To love your neighbor is to send out a feeler, a spiritual wire of Good Will toward him. In due time he will feel that feeler and connect with it, and there you have your rapport.

The second requisite for giving and receiving conscious telepathic messages is definiteness of thought. I once saw in a New York paper some pictures made by photographing thoughts. One of these pictures represented the Flatiron Building. The building appeared as a wavering pillar of black smoke, with here and there near the top a few spots of light that represented windows.

Too many of our thoughts are too wavering and inaccurate to be recognized by the percipient. In telepathic experiments take simple things, observe them carefully, and picture them mentally in exact detail. In sending word messages speak the words very distinctly and slowly in your thought, repeating several times, spelling out carefully, following out each letter accurately as you spell, all without moving the lips. This is good mental practice and justifies the time spent, even if the results in message bearing are less than perfectly satisfactory.

Definiteness of thought will develop in you by practice in this way, and in other ways, and with every year you will find yourself growing more positive and exact and forceful in your thoughts, as well as more sensitive to the thoughts of others.

To receive another's thought sit quietly in the silence, let go, and be ready to receive. Practice will do the rest for you. So much for telepathy through personal rapport. Now let us sum up with a brief statement of the nature and uses of telepathy.

Just as there are two sorts of mind, conscious and subconscious, so there are two kinds of telepathy. One is subconscious and wireless, and practically beyond our control. Subconscious telepaths come to us incessantly from all directions. To all intents and purposes we swim in a sea of such messages.

And our subconsciousness takes in any of those messages which it is keyed to receive. Every ganglionic center in your body—beginning with the great sympathetic center, the solar plexus, which may be likened to New York City; from that on down to the smallest ganglion in your body, of which there are thousands, that may be likened to the little outlying country villages of our land;—every one of these centers is a marconigraph station, each keyed by you to receive certain messages from the atmospheric and etheric vibrations in which you live.

And this is not all: every cell in your body is an individual receiver of messages on its own account. And each and every cell acts upon its messages received, even as you and I.

Each receiving ganglion and cell is keyed by you. Remember that. How to do the keying we shall learn later.

Now note that all this receiving of messages by the 95 per cent, self of you is done under your conscious mind, outside it. But the reports on those messages come up to the 5 per cent, conscious self of you, by way of the nerves.

All this bears exact analogy to the work of ex-President Roosevelt's commission on the prevention of cruelty to farmers and their wives. The commission did outside of Washington, which stands for the head, all their work of receiving messages from the farmer in the 95 per cent, self of our country; afterward collating and coordinating those messages and reporting the resulting opinions back to the conscious U. S. self represented by Congress. It now remains for Congress to key this country so that its next messages from the farmers will report better things.

Note that Washington does not hear and know when you and I get messages from over in England or Germany; it is not informed when we thresh out our discontents in town meetings and local clubs; but the consensus of these things it receives in Congress, the conscious U. S. self, through the regular channels. And Washington on its own account receives messages from foreign countries which do not come by the subconscious route;

just as you and I receive occasionally a conscious telepathic message.

Telepathy is a natural power of every human being, used in the main unconsciously, or rather subconsciously; but susceptible of development on the conscious plane, through aspiration, concentration, definiteness of thought, and practice.

10

MENTAL IMMIGRATION.

WE are all destined to come into rapport with the whole world through the wireless medium of the cosmic consciousness. Always this rapport has been ours subconsciously. We have ever lived in a sea of messages coming to us from those about us, and from those who lived and thought before us and went away leaving the air charged with their messages.

We are heirs to all the ages of thought, and we are living in and by a sea of thought which we draw upon subconsciously but none the less effectually. This great sub-surface reservoir of ourselves composes about 95 per cent. of us, and through it we have been receiving and are receiving, and acting upon, ten thousand telepathic messages from all corners of earth and heaven— messages we receive as coming in most cases from within ourselves but which really come from without and are received by us.

There is no way of deciding how many of our actions and feelings are due to this subconscious reception of telepathic messages, but it is safe to say that somewhere about half or three quarters or more of our feelings and actions are thus stimulated from without.

So large is the proportion that some scientists have declared we are altogether the product of our environment, and these same scientists looked wholly upon the physically traceable part of our environment at that.

Their instruments failed to measure the telepathic, the occult forces of our environment. It took the twentieth century to develop man to the point of glimpsing this unseen and potent side of life, which the greatest scientists are now investigating.

And in the meantime you and I and they have been growing in wisdom and knowledge and wickedness mainly by receiving and acting upon these same subconscious telepaths; calling the impulse our own.

They are "our own," in the sense that we are all one, using the same air, light, sunshine/wisdom, God, the same psychic and mental atmosphere to grow in and by. They are "our own" impulses in exactly the same way that the center of the star is each point's own center. By that same token do you see why it is so hard for one of us to be fully saved from sin, sickness, death, untrue thought, until all are saved? All the time we are receiving some measure of impulse toward these things by subconscious telepathy.

But there is a way, and that way is indicated by the latest invention of the wireless telegraph, that enables a receiving station; to be so keyed that it will fail to pick up messages in other keys. Every individual has the key of this problem within himself. He can key himself to any pitch he desires, so that thought waves of certain other pitches will pass by unrecorded.

The emotions or sympathies are what decide our pitch. They are the life of the subconscious 95 per cent. self of us, and upon their pitch depends the kind of thought vibrations we answer to in spite of ourselves and all our high purposes and conscious desires.

These emotions and sympathies constitute what the Bible calls "the heart." What a man is keyed to in his heart determines what he attracts as environment and heart impulse. And remember—environment includes that subconscious sea of telepathic messages, race beliefs, heredities in which we live and by which we are subconsciously impelled.

Herein lies the reason that the magnet man does not always attract what he is conscious of desiring. His conscious desire may be at cross-purposes with his subconscious desire. And the subconscious self, you know, weighs nineteen times as much as the conscious self! No wonder its desires rule. No wonder its keynote counts in the harmonies or discords of your life.

But that little 5 per cent. self of you is mighty. It is "God in the Highest" of you. It is "Lord God" of you, and of the Bible; and it is given all power in your subconscious self, as well as in your conscious self.

That little 5 per cent. self it is which keys your emotions and sympathies to their message-receiving work. That little 5 per cent. self is mightier than all below it, and its WORD is LAW. Even its idle word is law,— makes its subconscious mark upon you and keys you to more idle words. And these idle words have life in themselves and attract after their kind.

The idle words, like the good words, and the evil words, each attracts after its kind, and each builds up its Marconi station in you, keyed to messages of its kind.

You are like the United States, and your 5 per cent, conscious self is a sort of Ellis Island. The good, bad, and indifferent from all the world appear at Ellis Island, are inspected, some turned back, others invited to come in and settle. Those who are allowed to come in go and settle where there are others of their kind. Some get by on false pretenses. Others are turned back because the inspectors at Ellis Island misjudge, or because a prejudice—a pre-judgment —excludes them, as in the case of certain anarchists. So you sit at your Ellis Island and ten thousand thoughts pass in review before you.

And some you turn back, for good reason or for prejudice, and they go their way leaving you untouched, unchanged. And some thoughts you invite in and entertain, and they go their way into the big America of your 95 per cent. sub-self, and there they find a congenial settlement where they make their homes, breed after their kind, and receive and act upon outside telepaths of their sort.

But most of the thoughts that pass your Ellis Island are of the kind you call indifferent—neither good nor bad, just so-so; good as most people's thoughts, you guess; "good enough," "harmless anyway"; and these you let in, too, and they find congenial thought towns and settle there, breeding after their kind and receiving and sending subconscious telepaths to match. And some of your settlements of thoughts are good and make you feel good; and others are evil and give you evil feelings; and some of them settle in slums, and make you feel very bad indeed when you are conscious of them at all!

And your little Ellis Island did it all! If you didn't exactly create your subconscious America, at least you invited folks in to settle it, and its government and its evils as well as its blessings are the natural inevitable result, with nobody to blame but yourself. And you are not to blame because you didn't know any better and you are learning by experience.

So now you are going to be very strict on your Ellis Island hereafter! No more criminals or incompetents are to get in—that's decided! You will turn the undesirables back with a denial and welcome the desirables with a yes, an affirmation.

But what to do with the ones already in, that's the question! How shall you go about it to get yourself keyed above all these settlers that seem planted and so persistent in increasing and multiplying after their kind, and so determined to smuggle in other influences of their kind by the subconscious telepathic route?

11

ACTION AND REST

POSITIVE affirmation is the mandate that keys your body; just as the mandates sent out by Congress key the United States.

But one must do something besides issue laws to his being, and command his thought-people to carry out the laws. He must also rest from his mental labors of lawmaking and give his thought-people, conscious and subconscious, plenty of time for rest and recreation. "God giveth to his beloved in sleep." Man gives out his thought-force and emotion while he thinks and works, and he must have the rest of change and of sleep or it will be all giving out, until he is powerless to give further.

Action must alternate with rest, inspiration with expiration; and it is up to you as the lawmaker of your being to see that every cell of your body gets its full meed of rest and change. And how are you to know how much rest your bodily functions need, as a whole or in part? Only by listening to their report. The joy of being is the proof that you are not overworking at least a part of your organization of little cell beings. To keep a good "head of vim" as Stephens calls it—a good head of joy vim—is the only safe and sane and sure way to "enjoy God." And that is your chief end in life.

It is true that once in a while you can keep on working until you get your second wind, or your third wind. But you can't keep on living on your second or third wind, and the man who tries to will come out as Dr. Worcester did. He will have to take a long rest to balance the long overworking on second wind.

The joy of living is the proof of right living—the proof that you are not making galley slaves of a large proportion of your little cell people. "'Shorter hours and better work" for your energies is the law of Tightness in you as well as in the commercial world. Just as wise business men nowadays look after the clean living, education, and recreation of their workmen, so you must look after the needs and desires of your little thought-people. You stand in relation to your cell lives and energies exactly as God stands in relation to you. Don't be an exacting and slave-making god! Love your energies, joy in them, keep them well recreated by rest and by change of work.

Do not try to pass fatigue barriers! What's the use of it? Keep a good head of joy-vim every day and all day and you will do better work and more of it, and be in better trim to get your second wind or third wind if sometime it be- comes a real necessity to endure a strain.

Take kindly wise care not to overwork any part of your body. Don't make a mill hand of yourself with long hours of work without thought and love. And don't let too much of your thought evaporate out of the top of your head while your body idles. Direct much of your thought through your body in intelligent work, but don't pass the fatigue barrier in any one kind of work unnecessarily. Let go and change when your body begins to want to. Your instinct is the true guide in this —trust it and keep on. Practice makes perfect and develops power.

To exercise all parts of the body and mind in turn, always changing the field of exercise before the joy of being—not joy of doing—has been lowered, is to fulfill the chief end of man, which is the enjoyment of Good, or God. But all this must come from an inner heart impulse, not from a mere dead head plan.

To love the thing you do is necessary to enjoying it and God.

And to do it for a purpose larger than that of mere personal development is an absolute demand of the God in you. You are a member of "one Stupendous Whole" whose soul is your soul; and this soul of you cannot be satisfied except yourself is developed, not for you alone, but for the good of the whole.

Useful work for the good of others is the demand of your being, and without it you can't enjoy God in you, no matter how systematically you may exercise your energies.

A POLARIZING PURPOSE IS AN INHERENT DEMAND OF YOUR BEING.

To really enjoy living you must work for others, and do it in such a way that your own development will come through your useful work for others. If you run a grocery store with the primary purpose of getting money for yourself you cannot fully enjoy the work nor God in it. If your primary purpose is the real artist's purpose of supplying people's wants in the best possible manner at fair prices, there is only one thing can spoil your enjoyment of God in the work, and that is, lowering your head of joy-vim by too steady application without change for re-creation. If you love your work and work at it intelligently, not immoderately, you help the world along and develop yourself at the same time.

And if your recreations are well chosen, affording complete relaxation from business thoughts and the interested activity of entirely different thought-areas and muscle-areas, your development will be so much the more rapid and complete and soul-enjoying.

The soul-satisfying life is one of all-around activity and development, the life of poise—the natural life, the simple life, the life in which relaxation equals application, and where, no matter how complex the mode of living, mind and body are free to turn readily and with joy from one thing to another. Our old conception of life is a straight line, a strain ahead; now we are learning that it is a poise, a balance of thinking and doing that releases love in every activity.

Does all this sound complex? It is really very simple—it means simply let go mentally, and follow desire. It means believe that God desires in you, and that by following desire you will learn to fulfill the chief end of man, enjoyment of God, or Good.

If there is strain in your life it comes from an unnatural idea of life. Don't try to live up to anything—let go and let the impulse from within move you to every action. Otherwise, don't act. Accept the inner impulse as good, no matter how it may seem to disagree with your old man-made ideas of duty.

This new way of taking your good- ness for granted and living from the inner impulse may turn your living upside down for a time. When I came to see the artificialness and strain of my life (some fifteen years ago) and let go, I went to sleep for three weeks! Waked up and felt "I ought"— Affirmed myself good, and my sleep impulse good, turned over and went to sleep again. In between sleeps I did what was absolutely necessary to keep others in the home from starving.

At last one afternoon came a real desire to get up and clean up the kitchen and get a nice dinner! Ever after I laid for my desire-impulse, followed as far as it moved me, then rested again while another desire brewed within me.

The result was (1) the real enjoyment of good in working out the impulse; (2) increasing faith and proof that my desire-impulses were right guides to action, and the lack of them the right signal for inaction; (3) an increasing number of these desire-impulses from within, with increasing physical energy to carry them out. Right impulse—and peace of mind— and physical force came to me through trusting and acting with my own desire impulses and now-impulses as the voice of God within me. I found the kingdom of heaven within me, where life-impulse is generated, and made my thoughts and actions right with it. All other things were promptly added. Health of self came first, but not complete health. Work-impulse came, with power to do.

The desire to heal others came, and with it the power. That desire came before I was healed myself, altogether; and I found self-healing came faster if I healed others, and that my limitations did not hinder other people from responding to my "perfect word."

How I used the subconscious in many healings of others in the family and neighborhood; how I became a sun center of healing and discovered and applied several new principles of spiritual healing are told in my little "Experiences in Self-Healing" and "How to Wake the Solar Plexus," and need not be repeated here. I

56

found the healing of others the best practice for personal healing and power and development.

Always begin treatments for self or others with (1) meditation; (2) then full breathing; (3) then denials if needed; (4) then positive affirmations, repeated; (5) then silence, which may terminate in sleep.

12

THE PRACTICE OF PROSPERITY.

MAN is a magnet. To be opulent within is to charge one's self with the magnetism that attracts friends, ideas, money. The right attitude of mind will bring wealth through any business channel that does not run counter to the individual's belief in right.

First, choose the business you desire, the one you feel fitted for or specially adapted for. If you can't choose—just now—then adapt yourself to the business you find yourself in. To love your work, those you meet, yourself, and your methods and goods, is absolutely essential to growing a success. These may all become irksome, after your successful business is established, and your success still goes on; but to create a successful business you must put into its every detail unlimited quantities of loving interest and thought. It is easier to generate the loving interest if you can choose your work; but it is quite possible to do it in any business by which you can serve man's real needs.

I doubt if a new thought man can succeed as a saloon keeper, because saloons pander to that which destroys man, not builds him; and knowledge of this fact takes the heart out of the saloon man who learns that all men are his brothers.

To grow success, begin where you must, if not where you would like to. Put your loving thought into making the greatest possible artistic success of each detail of the work as it comes up. A big success is made up of ten thousand little successes of detail, all pieced together with faith and love for the work as a whole.

The spirit in you is the only reliable guide to your successful business as a whole. Ask yourself what you can begin on now to grow success. The thing lies straight before you in the thing you can do or are doing now— unless your spirit is urging you to some certain definite step into something else. When the spirit of you urges a definite step, take it; until then put your love into making successes every hour right where you are.

To make a hundred detail-successes a day where you are, and to use some of your recreation time and thought in preparing yourself with a good stock of tools to work with in some new line toward which your being inclines you, is the road to the sort of success your being calls for.

But remember that your chief end is to enjoy good in every day and hour of work. Put your loving interest into the now, and ask your spirit for light on how to arrange your details so as to get out of them quickest results in joy and growth.

Ask your desire-spirit these things, and follow its urge in faith. Do not ask your neighbors or friends, or your own sense of conventions. Follow your desire-impulse and have faith in results. Shut your eyes and ears from hearing of criticisms, except from your desire-self.

Practice proves. You are the worker-out of your successes. Nobody can help you except as they can perchance supply you a tool to work with. You must use the tool. Education supplies tools to you. Your friend may teach you bookkeeping, for instance, and you use it or not, as your desire-urge directs.

But conventions are not tools! they are ruts made by other men. Use them when it makes easier going, but when your desire-urge prefers a new path, a short cut, for God's sake take it. Only so can you make tracks of your own in the sands of time. Be the real thing by following your own desire-urge into new ways. Who knows but the world needs your new ways ? And anyway you need them to fulfill the chief end of your being here at all.

To love your work; to follow your desire in growing it; to use tools, methods, as your desire urges; to use common sense in all things; to be just to yourself in money matters before you are lavish with the other man; to count in all the costs and allow yourself a fair profit above everything; to pay cash and require cash (or as near it as possible); to make due allowance everywhere for the Unexpected; to manage always a savings balance accumulated for the Day of Opportunity; to do all this in joy; to grow in wisdom and in knowledge and in loving-kindness by doing it; and by doing it to help and bless the world you live in;—these constitute the Successful Life every soul desires. And every soul can work it out if he will trust his own inner urge and value his joy of being above all material results. The treatment for success is the same as for health; repeated affirmations, present tense, positive mood. I AM what I desire to manifest.

Do not try to influence others—be and do the thing that attracts you. Remember—success, like heaven, is an attitude of mind that is creating a local habitation. Success comes first in thought, and as the thought pattern appears, Love creates in its image and likeness. Read "The Science of Getting Rich," by Wallace D. Wattles, and my own "How to Grow Success," and "How to Wake the Solar Plexus" and "Experiences in Self-Healing." The latter contains my own experiences in outgrowing poverty.

13

THE PRINCIPLES AND PRACTICE OF HEALTH AND PROSPERITY.

I WONDER if you are now realizing the great truth that this universe is a big Living, Loving Presence that feels and thinks and loves through you and in you. And that the chief end of you is to be the glory of this Presence, and enjoy it forever.

To know thyself is to know the Divine Presence and its ways within you. And the way to this knowledge and illumination is the way of aspiration and inspiration; the way of communion with the One Loving Presence; the way of dedication and consecration; the way of resignation to the will of the One Presence, trusting that step by step the wisdom of the One Presence will reveal itself.

Solomon's prayer is the only availing one: "Give therefore thy servant an understanding heart." It is not enough to pray for, or aspire to, wisdom, unless one is first given over to be the servant of that wisdom. And neither is it enough to ask wisdom for self alone, for wisdom is One, and grants no favors to you that are disfavors to your neighbor.

Not until your very subconscious center is given over to desiring the good of all can you come into real rapport with the Love Presence, so that the real joy as well as the wisdom of it is yours. You cannot enjoy God, the Loving Presence, except you glorify and exalt it above everything, above YOURSELF. Resignation, consecration, aspiration, then exaltation of spirit. After this all things shall be added. And the work is all done in your thought.

Remember that your thought keys your body.

This does not mean that the body is nothing and has no effect on thought, that thought is all there is to it. Thought is not a vaporous nothing thrown off by the body; thought is of the same identical material as the body. The body is congealed thought, and that which we commonly call thought is positive to the body, and acts upon it.

Thought is to the body what steam is to ice.

Thought is like steam generated in a boiler and turned to moving our bodies intelligently.

Think a moment: What part of your body can control a thought in your mind? Can your whole body put a thought out of your mind? No. Your entire body may be so paralyzed it cannot act, and yet there will be thoughts in your mind.

But a single thought of your mind can move your body in any direction; a joy thought can galvanize it to life; a fear thought can stop its machinery forever. Just one thought can make or unmake a body, but a hundred bodies cannot stop a thought, once recognized. But this does not mean that thought and body are separate things, any more than it means that thought is powerless or the body no matter. It just means that without thought man falls down and scrambles on all fours; that thought is the wisdom-power that directs the action and evolution of body, and without it we revert to imbeciles and idiots.

No, it is not the body that makes the idiot; his mother's thought ran amuck somewhere and pied her unborn babe's poor little thought-built but negative body, so that the real self cannot think through it. The idiot's body is an incomplete thing that limits the expression of its thought. For, though the body cannot control thought because it is negative to the thought that expresses through it, yet it can limit the output of thought, just as a small or incomplete flour mill can limit the output of flour. The mill does not regulate the supply of wheat to be made into flour, but its capacity determines the amount and quality of flour it can turn out.

In the case of the mill, both mill and wheat are negative, having no effect in changing each other. But the human thought mill, the complete body including its brain, is very greatly affected by the thought it turns out.

This is fact beyond peradventure of doubt; and this one fact looks to me like proof positive that both brain and thought are developed and used by a YOU that is positive to both; that stands in relation to brain, body, and thought as the mill man to mill and wheat; is positive to both, and changes and improves both as fast as he can to increase size and quality of output.

It looks to me as if this positive YOU is the evolutionary energy of the universe, and is identical with "the unknown God" that Paul tried to "declare" unto the Athenians, and that ecclesiastics and layman teachers have been trying to understand and declare ever since.

That body and brain are used by an unseen power that calls itself I, or I AM THAT I AM, or I AM WHAT I AM DECLARING, AND THEN SOME! is to me a proved assumption even without the dicta of scientists. I feel and KNOW, by observation and introspection, that I use my body and my brain, that I call up new thoughts; that I command them. And Victor Hugo knew this when he wrote in his later years those immortal words which find echo in many hearts:—

"I feel in myself the future life. I am like a forest once cut down; the new shoots are stronger and livelier than ever. I am rising, I know, toward the sky. The sunshine is on my head. The earth gives me its generous sap, but heaven lights me with the reflection of unknown worlds.

"You say the soul is nothing but the resultant of the bodily powers. Why, then, is my soul more luminous when my bodily powers begin to fail? Winter is on my head, but eternal spring is in my heart. I breathe at this hour the fragrance of the lilacs, the violets, and the roses as at twenty years. The nearer I approach the end the plainer 1 hear around me the immortal symphonies of the worlds which invite me. It is marvelous, yet simple. It is a fairy tale, and it is history.

"For half a century I have been writing my thoughts in prose and in verse; history, philosophy, drama, romance, tradition, satire, ode, and song; I have tried all. But I feel I have not said the thousandth part of what is in me. When I go down to the grave I can say like many others, I have finished my day's work.' But I cannot say, I have finished my life.' My day's work will begin again the next morning. The tomb is not a blind alley; it is a thoroughfare. It closes on the twilight, it opens on the dawn"

The fact that brain, body, and thought do not always obey me proves not that I am less I, but that the brain and body and every thought I have called into being are endowed with volition and wisdom of their own within and by me, that every thought is a mental creature with will of its own, created under and subject to those same seven principles elucidated in the first three chapters of this book.

The unruliness of my thoughts and of my thought-made body only proves that they are alive in their own right; that the kingdom I am trying to rule is a kingdom of living beings, not of dead putty.

But there are other proofs that I and my thoughts are one in exactly the same sense that the Father and I are one; that my body and my thoughts are literally my alive body and my living thoughts—not me myself.

For formal scientific proof that your body and brain are your instruments, not you, con William Hanna Thomson's "Brain and Personality."

For present purposes let us assume this to be true: That you act upon your body to produce -conscious thought, which, in turn, acts within your body to produce a finer body, and, in turn, still finer thought.

If we assume this or accept it as proved, we cannot evade seeing the point that the thoughts in our minds are the only thing we need be solicitous about. If we let only desirable thought-people through our mental Ellis Island gate we need not tag around after them to see that they do no harm. -We can sit serene and trust them to settle where attraction takes them, and get busy about their work of improving conditions within us.

In other words, we think the WORD into our cosmos and it straightway makes its mark there, after its kind, The United States let in a generation or two ago, a Word, a man named Roosevelt. Uncle Sam didn't tag him with policemen to keep him out of mischief. And from this man's natural activities came good work, marriage, children, grandchildren, Theodore Roosevelt and the imprint for good which he has made. All from one little man let in.

This is an exact parallel and not at all an exaggeration of the power the right sort of thought exerts to make its mark on your body. Yes, an exact parallel ; for your thought-words form the cells or families of your body, and these increase and multiply and work and think, and wield an influence on the whole body, just as people do in the whole world.

The same laws work everywhere in every atom and cell.

So right living resolves itself into right thinking. It resolves itself into a matter of Good Government of Thought-People; a government that lets in the best thoughts to settle your body and improve it; a government that looks to the needs of all its settlers, that conserves and develops its natural resources; that educates every one of its people and gives everyone its opportunities and responsibilities in helping along the whole; a government of the head that despises no part as common, that HONORS the hand, the foot, the excretory organs, the sex organs, too, and develops each for the good of all.

Eugenics as well as hygienics must rule within the personal body if it is ever to rule within the world. Now the question is, how shall we get our kingdom in order?

We cannot kill off all the evil and false thoughts we have let in in the past any more than we can kill off all the negroes and Indians and criminals and incompetents and hobos in our United States and give the country over to the nice, cultured, respectable folk.

Only one course is open to the individual and the nation alike: To admit hereafter only desirable thoughts and people; to educate to useful service every one already within the gates; to restrain and educate the lawless; and to patiently trust the rest to that law of nature which says the "wicked shall not live out half their days" while the "righteous shall inherit the earth."

And that last clause is the most important one of the three, and the first. For without trust in the law of good—the evolutionary principle of nature, if you prefer that term,—without trust in God as the power that is working all things for good and better, and best, as the religionist says; without this faith in the outcome of effort no government could make the effort to keep out the undesirable invader, or to educate to useful service those already within its borders. Nor could the individual without trust in this same law in himself ever muster up the energy to perform the same service for his thought-built body.

Lack of faith in the One Living Presence and the Law of Evolution is the cause of pessimism. "Pessimism is a disease," Horace Fletcher says It is. Pessimism is creeping paralysis, and its cure is faith and work. At Ellis Island they have a set of definite rules by which they judge an immigrant before they let him through the gates.

So you and I need a principle by which to judge the thoughts we allow in our minds. The best rule I know of is given in one of Paul's epistles—"the fruit of the spirit is love, joy, peace, longsuffering (or patience), gentleness, goodness, faith, meekness (meekness of a child), temperance (in all things); against such there is no law."

So thoughts that bring love, joy, peace, patience, gentleness, meekness, goodness, faith, and temperance are to be invited into our minds and given every encouragement to dwell within us and increase and multiply and take care of themselves, and glorify and beautify and healthify us.

When you are in doubt about a thought measure it by all nine of these words and turn it back if it isn't up to standard.

Is it a loving thought? Is it a thought that radiates joy? or peace? Sometimes you can't see the joy in a new thought that comes up, but you can always tell whether its entrance would bring peace. Is it a thought that brings patience? gentleness? meekness? goodness? Is it a thought that brings a temperate feeling? Above all, is it a thought shod with faith—faith in God within you, and God within the other man? If the thought can honestly answer yes to this quiz, open wide the gate and let him in.

If he can't, turn him back to the bottomless pit whence he came. But don't worry if he refuses to get out of your sight, or if he keeps coming back again. Keep turning him down until he gets discouraged and quits coming!

And the best way to keep him from coming up before your gate is to turn your back on him and get busy with thoughts that can pass the quiz with plenty of room to spare.

The gate within you is the gate of CHOICE, or Will. You can choose your gate open to a thought, or you can choose it shut! The thought, being alive on its own account, may hang around if you choose to shut the gate in its face, but it cannot get into you or hurt you until you choose to let it.

Your choice is the one mighty little bit of your being over which you have absolute control. "Choose ye this day whom ye will serve." Choose you this moment what thought you will invite in.

Practice in choosing the right thought makes perfect; and by and by your body and brain will be so settled and governed by the right thoughts that unright ones will cease to besiege you for admission. For the law of attraction works here, you know,—to him who hath been settled up by evil thoughts shall more evil thoughts come. Hobos avoid certain well governed towns in Massachusetts as they would a pestilence; so will hobo thoughts avoid the mind that is positive to them.

Here come in the positive and negative attitudes of mind that puzzle so many people. Choice is the gate which, closed, makes you positive, and opened, negative.

You cannot stand ever at that gate, waking and sleeping, to guard the entrance, any more than Congress can stand ever at Ellis Island judging immigrants. But you can do within yourself exactly what Congress does—issue a man- date that will cause certain sets of brain cells within you to perform that office. You never see those cells any more than Congress sees the inspectors at the island, but they are appointed to their work just the same, and they are just as faithful at the work as the steady positiveness of your mandate requires. You are the lawgiver of your being, and at your command are all the competent officers needed for the work, and all the police and detective and navy organizations needed to see that they do it.

Not a function or functionary in public government but has its exact analogy within you.

I wish you would read in this connection several chapters on cell life and organization in C. A. Stephens "Natural Salvation." The ultimate conclusions in that book are shortsighted, it seems to me, but the scientific description of the human organization is wonderfully vivid and exact.

You can send into your being a positive mandate to invite in the thoughts that can stand that quiz and to turn back the thoughts that can't; you can reiterate that mandate positively, calmly, firmly, at certain set periods every day, never minding it much between times; and if you are faithful at the practice you are just as dead sure to see results in due time as the world is to see the flowers bloom in the spring, —and by the self-same law of growth.

Patient, persistent reiteration sent into your body will just as surely take root and grow and produce after its kind as orange seeds will grow if planted in the right place.

And I don't care whether you have faith in the practice or not. Faith is necessary to the process, but if you have faith enough to keep you at the practice, that faith will grow like any other planted seed, and in time you will have all the faith you know what to do with.

To do the thing plants your grain of faith, and the natural law of growth takes care of the rest. Whatsoever things you desire you can manifest in your body by sending forth your mandates in LOVE, JOY, PEACE, PATIENCE, FAITH, TEMPERANCE, and trusting the life in you to do the rest.

There is nothing good that you can imagine for our people of the United States that cannot be worked out by those people, if you give them time and good mandates to work by. The gates of hell and Ellis Island cannot and will not prevent.

If you have the seership of the cosmic consciousness you know all good is being worked out among us, and your joy and enthusiasm and love grow with the thought.

Even so within you is all good being worked out. You are building better than you know. Your ideals and desires are YOU, and unceasingly they are working themselves out within and through you as within the world.

Wake up now, and accept your good for granted, and work consciously for it and with it. Take your dominion in the only place you can, in your thoughts, and the spirit of all life will do the rest.

14

INTERACTION OF MIND AND BODY.

WE all want, first, to be delivered from sin and sickness; then from poverty. I think I have shown you by antithesis that sin is merely a falling short of the ideal which is our higher, positive self, and which constitutes our conception of what we and our doings "ought" to be. As our ideal grows larger our conception of what constitutes sin changes.

Always that "ought" urges us to live up to our ideal, and this we cannot always do because our ideal is ever ahead of our ability to make real. Until we understand this and forgive ourselves for our shortcomings we are destined to writhe under that sense of sin. Until we do understand ourselves and our relation to the One Life we think it is God's forgiveness we are after—God outside ourselves.

To supply this need of forgiveness came Jesus and other saviors, who knew themselves as one with the Father, and who in his name rolled that paralyzing burden of sin from the hearts of the self-ignorant ones.

This was an expedient necessary and aidful until man's intelligence should develop to the point of finding God in his own heart, the God of love and wisdom—not of anger and revenge—ready to forgive his every shortcoming, and ever urging him on to fresh effort.

The "ought" in every human heart is certain to create a sense of sin or shortcoming, and this sin must find some sort of forgiveness, or hope dies and there is no joy in effort. Forgiveness of sin is necessary. "God was in Christ Jesus reconciling the world unto himself"—not reconciling himself unto the world, as the sin-burdened one naturally supposed. Until the sin-burdened one was reconciled he was too discouraged to try again to live up to that ideal of his of what he "ought" to be and do. Forgive yourself through knowing yourself. Choose to admit and to Godspeed thoughts of self-forgiveness. But remember that to forgive yourself you must first forgive all others. Non-forgiveness expresses in tension and fear, no matter whether it is non-forgiveness of self or of somebody else! "To know all is to forgive all."

Know yourself and all others as incomplete and growing expressions of GOD, and you can forgive all shortcomings. To do this, take those Twelve Planks of the New Thought Platform into the silence with you and live with them. Do it every day. Take one plank at a time and live with it, meditate over it, pray with it, think by it, for a week. Take special periods two or three times a day for "holding the thought" stated, holding the thought quietly, waiting and listening for the One Spirit's illumination of the text. At the end of a week take up the next plank in the same way. Follow this up with the whole twelve statements. By the end of the twelve weeks' faithful work you will find it no effort to forgive yourself and all the world.

And most, if not all, your diseases will disappear with your grudges, your unforgivingnesses. For hard feelings are at the bottom of all dis-eases, if they are not indeed the only thing at the bottom of them. For hard feelings are literally hardening of the feelings and of the whole nervous system; and this is the beginning of all disease.

Hard feelings result in hardening of the nerves, then of the arteries. These eventuate in shutting off blood supply in some portion or portions of the body, and inflammations, tumors, cancers, and what not appear. So disease grows from the mere disease of hard feelings to the violent pains of approaching disintegration. And mind you, thoughts, HARDENING thoughts, are at the bottom of it all. THE CURE is softening thought, thoughts that wake love, joy, peace, faith in God, men and self; thoughts of patience, gentleness, temperance. "Love your enemies, do good," is the new thought specific for sin, sickness, poverty, and death itself.

As to specific ways of treating disease, there are many; and the best formula for you to use is your formula, not mine. And indeed I have no formula; I use the thought that comes up to my mind in connection with any particular case, always taking care to state it in the positive mood, present tense. This is what Paul Militz used to call the "perfect word,"—the statement that the thing is complete now.

"I am going to be well," will keep you going, but never arriving. "I AM WHOLE NOW," backed by temperate action, and persistently used, will do the work.

The same perfect word may be applied to any specific part of the body that happens to be specially hardened and diseaseful, as well as to your being as a whole.

All scientists agree to-day that "the blood is the life of the flesh," as somebody said in the Old Testament. All up-to-date doctors diagnose by blood tests. They measure the quality of the blood through a magnifying glass; and the pressure of the blood, which latter indicates accurately the degree of hardening of arteries, through either nerve tension or calcareous deposit. And all advanced doctors aim first and last and all the time to make rich blood and to keep blood pressure normal.

That they depend wholly upon drugs to do this is their misfortune and the patients'. But even this is passing the calamity stage through the new movement of Dr. Cabot and others beginning in Boston to develop a sort of Emmanuel movement of their own, teaching their patients how to substitute right thinking and right living for drugs. The mental scientist says that right thinking and feeling is the one essential for health.

The physical scientist says all diseases are blood diseases and that pure blood well circulated is the one essential. But I say unto you that both these things are equally essential to a sound mind and body. And I say also that neither one can exist without the other; that right thinking and pure blood act and react upon each other; that whatever affects one has its equal effect upon the other. Soul, brain, and body are one, built of one substance.

At Yale the professors and students do much experimenting with a contrivance called a muscle bed. It consists of a six-foot table poised as delicately as a druggist's scales. A man lies full length on this table exactly in the center, so that the ends are evenly balanced. The professor gives him a difficult problem to solve mentally. He figures away in his mind. After a moment the head of the table tilts slowly downward. The effort of thinking out that problem draws the blood to his head and the delicate scales show it.

Then the table is balanced exactly again for another trial. "Now think of your feet," says the professor. The man thinks steadily of his feet. After a moment, slowly downward tilts the foot of the table. The blood increases in his feet when he thinks steadily of them.

This indicates to you why mental treatments for a special organ or nerve center are effective. The blood and the Word work together right at the point where special effort is needed.

You can think the blood into any part of your body, and the blood will carry food to that part, and carry the refuse and poison out of that part. Remember that blood itself is thought-made and thought-directed; it is subconscious thought in its nature; and that your conscious thought is always the mandate giver for your subconscious thought-people. To liken the leucocytes or phagocytes of the blood to policemen is truth, not metaphor.

Speak the perfect Word for your body as a whole, and for each part that seems to need special care, and trust the little blood-people to do your bidding. And right here we come to the physical side of life, which it is foolishness to try to ignore. Blood may be purified or contaminated by thought; it may be made sluggish or swift-running by thought; but it may also be contaminated or purified, its circulation accelerated or retarded by physical means.

And Life says there are distinct limits beyond which mind cannot go without body, nor body without mind. To prove this quickly you have only to shut yourself up in the bath room, plug up the keyhole, batten down the window, and turn on the gas. Then think your hardest and best, and see what good it will do you. A half hour of this will convince your friends if not you.

Do you see that exercise of the body is absolutely essential, or thinking must come to a stop sooner or later? Breathing is exercise of the body. Breathing is the one thing you MUST do if you are to live and think at all.

And evidently you must have the right kind of air to breathe, or you can't breathe long anyway. Shut up in the bath room with the gas turned on, all your thinking and your will can't keep you breathing but a few minutes. And your conscious thinking will stop long before your breathing does. Ever see a person die of asphyxiation?—long after he ceases to be conscious his labor and labor to get air into him.

Evidently there is something in the air we breathe without the constant USE of which we cannot think or live. The physical scientist says it is oxygen; I say it is oxygen and a number of finer ethers of which we as yet know little or nothing.

But the fact is the same in either event: that we must continuously inflate and deflate our bodies with air, or we can't think. So the bodily exercise of breathing is indispensable to the mental exercise of thinking, as well as vice versa.

C. A. Stephens says that consciousness and conscious thought are caused by a sort of bodily cosmic consciousness made by all the little cell-people of our nervous system "holding hands," as it were, in a continuous chain of mental activity of each cell for the good of the whole body.

Through our waking hours all our cell-people are attending to the business of the whole. Imagine the nerve cells "holding hands" and flashing messages from one to another through those held hands, each cell a specialist receiving and sending messages for the good of the whole, and you can perhaps grasp Mr. Stephens's idea of what consciousness consists of.

Now imagine all the little cell-people getting tired and quitting work at night, all letting go hands and each cell relaxing, resting, playing on its own account, cleaning out its little house, eating supper and going to bed—even as you and I after a day's work—imagine this and you will have a good idea of what takes place while we tire and go to sleep. In the waking time our body cells carry on the necessary work of the whole; while we sleep our cells carry on their own personal work, play, rest, recreate, sleep as they please and must.

Possibly our dreams are glimpses of little theatrical performances got up by some of our cell-people for their own amusement!

With this view of personal consciousness Mr. Stephens naturally admonishes you against giving your cell-people too long a day. He advises eight hours' sleep or more every night, good, sound sleep, induced by a hearty Godspeed to your little cell-people to run home now and enjoy themselves.

Other medical scientists claim to find what they call "fatigue poisons" generated by all kinds of effort, which poisons induce lethargy and sleep in the cells of the part exercised. According to them these fatigue poisons affect fully only the organs generating them, so the cells of one organ may sleep while those of another are fresh and active, and vice versa. This explains why our conscious minds sleep while our stomachs or other organs are working; and why one set of muscles rests while another is being exercised; why a brisk walk outdoors or a ten-minutes' breathing exercise corrects brain-fag.

According to this new thought of the medical scientist, the fatigue poisons are a beneficent provision of nature to make folks rest. During rest the poisons are all eliminated. Between you and me, I think those fatigue poisons are the natural excreta and effluvia of the little cell-people, and that they just let go hands and clean house after business hours, even as you and I.

The blood flow carries food to every part, organ, and cell of the body, and it carries off the sewage. This blood flow must be full, pure, and well circulated or there is trouble. The mind must do its share to regulate the blood, but it cannot do it all, as you proved in that closed bath room with the gas turned on.

Breathing is body exercise that keeps the blood flowing. The lungs have more to do with regulating circulation than the heart ha% as you can easily prove by a few exercises. Let the person with a "weak heart" practice breathing evenly, taking pains to make each exhalation as slow and even as the inhalation, and he will soon find his heart and circulation all right and his mind control much improved. William Hanna Thomson says insanity is a blood disease; and everybody knows when his blood gets thin and sluggish that his thoughts run like molasses in January, and his feelings are like wild chickens, fluttering, flying, foolish. When your blood is thin, no matter what the cause, you are negative to every germ that grows, and you can't even think straight.

Wrong thinking, lack of the right amount of body exercise to keep the blood booming on its course, lack of well masticated, nourishing food, or poisons, or germs,—these constitute the four sources of blood contamination. Any one or more or all of these causes may be active in any one case.

And if it is a chronic case you may safely bet that all the causes are active; for one cause cannot long live unto itself in the human organism. The whole thing gets out of order from soul to sole, and each and every part reacts on every other.

So good common sense tells you—does it not?—to eliminate so far as possible all four causes of poor blood supply. Regulate diet and exercise your jaws; exercise moderately every organ of the body, particularly your lungs; think a? highly and peacefully as you can. Send your mandate of health into all your mind and body; but give your little cell-people time to rest and regenerate themselves for the task you set them. The very first step to health is to take as few steps as possible, but let those be of the sort that will give your little cell people right conditions to work in.

The first need of the sick one is rest— absolute rest. Quit stuffing the stomach with anything until the cell-energies have time to throw out the "fatigue poisons," the decaying matter that is making them groan at their work.

Your energies need oxygen to burn up the germ-cultures within you, the dirt. Breathe, breathe good, fresh, oxygen-laden air. Breathing is the one exercise the sick man cannot overdo— unless he tries breathing foul air. Fresh air, outdoor air well breathed the sick man MUST have if he is ever to get rid of the poisons and germs that are killing him.

Water he must have, all he can take of it, to make his blood stream run free and to carry off the poisons. Food he should not have at all for several days, because it takes energy to digest and assimilate food, and the sick man's energy must go first for the cleaning out of the poisonous matter. A sick man's body is in the same condition that Messina was after the earth- quake—full of decaying cell-bodies that must be got rid of quick, a task that requires every energy and cries for more. Every man must be fed, yes, and every cell must be fed. But just as relief was rushed to Messina, so is relief rushed to diseased parts of the body from stores already on hand.

That is the real meaning of inflammation in the body—>a rush of blood and cell-people to clean up the trouble. Doctors now apply ice to regulate inflammation so the cell-people can work to better advantage—just as the government applied martial law to keep back the mobs of people who couldn't or wouldn't help clean up at Messina, and at San Francisco.

Mobs retard the work of cleaning up, and every atom of food above the line of absolute need does the same thing. Imagine the workers at Messina stopping to cook and eat three or four quails on toast apiece every day, to keep them from spoiling, and then taking the usual rest after a big meal, and you will see the point.

The food taken in by the sick man simply adds to the work and to the decaying heaps that must be disposed of, or pestilence gets in its work. Oxygen to make the fires burn up; water to keep the blood stream clear and flowing; lung exercise to keep the oxygen coming and the blood flowing; these are the indispensables to the sick man.

MIND DOES THE REST!

Do you see the point? If you are still inclined to quarrel with the use of physical means, answer me, please, this question: If mind is all, why not let mind do it all? Why insist upon helping mind by stuffing in food?

Why not cut off the densest of material aids, food, and let mind, air, and water do the work? Why not trust mind to call for food when she needs it? She certainly never calls for food in case of a really sick person. This ought to be a sufficient hint that she doesn't want it. Now let us get back to our center again.

The mind, or soul, or God runs the body by making it breathe in pure air and breathe out the effluvia and excreta of its countless billions of cell-people. The excretory organs get rid of unassimilated matter-food that was taken in without being properly prepared, or that was unneeded.

Here is prophecy: the time will come when man's digestive canal will be always as clean as the inside of a baby's mouth, and there will be no excreta; for we shall know better than to take into our stomachs more than we can excrete through lungs and pores. In due time our stomach and our bowels will follow our vermiform appendix and our coccyx into the bottomless pit of all useless things.

We eat air through lungs and pores; and in air is every constituent of foods. Why not do all our eating and excreting through lungs and pores,—as plants do? Why not eat air, drink water, and excrete perfume like the lily? It is desirable. And desire is true prophecy.

15

HOW TO LIVE A PERFECT DAY.

IF you were going to run a Marathon race would you prepare for it by sleeping until the last minute, then tumbling out of bed in a hurry, throwing on any old thing that came handy, and starting off at your highest possible speed? If you did you would certainly fall by the wayside before you had reached the halfway mark.

And yet to the average man and woman every day is a little Marathon race with Time, and many of us begin it in just that haphazard sort of hustle. If we don't hustle, we drag and complain, or we snap at every touch of those who are running the same little race beside us. When Hayes won the Marathon he trained for months before- hand. Every handicap of his living was laid aside; he ate the plainest food, kept regular hours, trained carefully every day, kept his mind ever polarized to the one thought of success in that race.

And because he made this careful preparation and ran the race in the most judicious fashion, beginning very easy and gaining speed as he progressed, he came out ahead of everybody else, still in good trim.

Dorando and others in the same race started out with the idea of distancing everybody in the first mile. For this one reason that they ran too hard at the beginning, they collapsed before they could reach the goal. They had spent their energy too lavishly at the start, while Hayes husbanded his.

The successful life is made up of a succession of successful days, every day being a little Marathon by itself. If we live a successful to-day, we make a wise preparation to live a successful to-morrow; and so on, day after day, year after year, through our whole lives.

Only to-day is ours. To-day we may make the right preparation, make the right and easy start, run the successful race with time, and close the day a victor. This day it is possible to do that. How shall we prepare for it? How husband our energies and direct our efforts? Let us begin the night before, by going to bed right, and at a reasonable hour. To go to bed right one should have fifteen minutes of quiet time for good reading, meditation, and affirmation before he closes his eyes.

Seat yourself comfortably and read a chapter in the best book you know of. Read slowly and meditate frequently. Get quiet, let go, and permit the Spirit to show you the real meaning of what you read. Aspire to know the truth, and remember that you are one with the Spirit of Truth, and that you make the connection by letting Truth into your thought, through aspiration and meditation.

Be still and know that I AM GOD. After reading, think over your day, and remember all the good things which have happened. If any unpleasant things come up accept their lesson, but deny their reality, deny their power, bid them begone and forgotten. Search for the good things in that day, and with every one that comes into your mind give thanks to the One Spirit which "worked in you to will and to do of his good pleasure." Invoke the Spirit to continue working within you, open your mind to It, love It. As you go to sleep remember that the One Spirit of love and wisdom and power enfolds you and moves through you while you sleep, cleansing, rejuvenating, reorganizing, getting you ready for the morrow. Tell yourself that you will sleep soundly, trustingly, well, and that you will wake in the morning, bright, interested, and full of power.

And in the morning. When you wake up, wake up. Rub your eyes promptly, stretch yourself with vigor and enjoyment for just half a minute, and then step resolutely to the floor. Do a few physical culture stunts to set your blood circulating. Take a few full breathing exercises before the open window. Bathe and dress properly and expeditiously. Concentrate on these things, and do them in the best possible manner, in the shortest possible time without hurrying.

If you have done these things with interest and good will, you have already performed half the work of getting your mind focused and directed for a successful day's work. Now complete your preparation by remembering again the one source from which you are to gain wisdom and power to make this the most happy and successful day of your life up to the present time. Thank this power for working in and through you, direct your mind to heed its promptings.

Read again for a few minutes from some high-potency book— perhaps the Bible, or Emerson.

Get your mind down to the now and remember that you are to begin easy, like the successful Marathon runner. If things go wrong, let them go. The only important thing to you is to keep going easy.

Someone has said that man is not fully civilized before ten o'clock in the morning. This means that he is either stupid or snappy until he gets well started for the day. These directions are intended to help you to concentrate on getting started right in fifteen or twenty minutes—to show you how to do in the first half hour of your day what most people require three to five hours to do. This gives you a longer day and higher potency without taking away from your sleeping hours.

After you have connected yourself in thought with the one source of wisdom and power and right direction, turn a few minutes of your time to planning your day. Divide your work up into essentials, and non-essentials, and frills. In the first division put those things which absolutely must be done, and along with them be sure to include several short rest periods for yourself, in which you are to again read high-potency books and reconnect yourself in thought with the one source of power and wisdom.

Be sure to put nothing in this division of essentials that can possibly be included as non-essentials or frills. In making this sort of division of your day, you get a better sense of proportion, and the things which are crowded out of the day will not burden, you with a subconscious sense of defeat.

Now you are properly prepared and directed for the day, body, mind, and soul. And you 'begin easy and gain impetus as the day goes. You likewise gain satisfaction as the day goes, because you find that each thing you do is done beautifully, i.e., it is done in the best possible manner, and the proof of it is in the sense of satisfaction which the thought of it wakes within you. Your day becomes a succession of things well done, and with every hour the sense of success, the sense of satisfaction, increases.

By night you may be tired, but your subconsciousness will be singing! In right doing there is great reward, and right doing is always proved step by step by that little subconscious "well done" which is the blessing of God within you.

When night time comes, remember to be grateful. Gratitude makes sure the connection between you and the one spirit of wisdom and power, love and joy. Be grateful for the power that enabled you to live a successful day. Commend yourself in peace to the one Spirit, to work within you its good will, while you sleep. Tell yourself that you are giving up soul, mind, and body to the workings of love and wisdom, and that you will wake up in the morning bright and interested and ready to advance.

Live one day at a time, live a successful day, and you will find each day a preparation in full for a better one coming. This is to live the life satisfying, the life useful and advancing.

I learned these things in the most expensive school— Experience. Much trouble of soul, great effort and thought and practice gave me the secret. I glory in it more every day of my life, and I pass the secret on to him who will use it. None other can take it!

16

THE SONG OF YOURSELF.

I THINK it is the Theosophists to whom we are indebted (?) for the idea that God is a very sublimated being a long way off, whose Lords rule over the solar systems in space, giving their commands to Mahatmas or something, some of whom dilute it and fix it up and pass it on down stingily to a few very uncommon mortals scattered over this earth, mainly in the Orient.

According to this philosophy the spirit is a long way removed from ordinary mortals, and the only wisdom that comes to mortals has to trickle down through beings of ever so many shades of superiority to said man. According to this theory (for it is only a theory and nothing else) God is too intangible and superior to have anything whatever to do with directing man. Mahatmas apparently amuse themselves with doling out wisdom when and where they see fit. And they get their wisdom from Lords higher up whose chief business in life is to dole out Lord-Wisdom to the Mahatmas. And so on, and so on, ad infinitum.

Why not have one anthropomorphic God and be done with it? Why have all these anthropomorphic Lords and Mahatmas between you and a sublimated God who cannot talk to you direct, and isn't interested in you anyhow? It seems to me this sort of theory is nothing in the world but a trituration of polytheism. We have pretended to outgrow polytheism and accept one God, but apparently some of us have only exchanged our poly-Gods for poly-Mahatmas, et al Right here I want to say that I don't believe in a poly-God. I believe in One God, who is just as close to me and to you as he is to any Mahatma or Lord in this universe, I don't care where he is nor whom.

I believe he speaks to us exactly as he did to Jesus of Nazareth. I believe that we live in him and by him.

"In him we live and move and have our being, and by him we consist." Take away God pure and simple, and there would be nothing left of you but a dead body—so dead that the worms couldn't eat it.

Bar God out of you and all the Mahatmas in Christendom couldn't even wiggle your little finger nor make you understand that black is black and white is white.

God is your life, your intelligence, your will, your love, your reality. Without God you would be a hole in space—if you can imagine such a thing. Without God you could not live, nor move, nor be.

God thought you into being and holds you there, and if all the Mahatmas and Lords in creation were swept into nothingness, God would keep on in-forming you until you grew into a new Mahatma and Lord bigger and better than any that have gone before. You can get away from the Mahatmas and Lords, you can do just as well without them.

But no matter whether you sit in heaven, walk on earth, or make your bed in hell, you cannot get away from God—there is a spiritual never-severed umbilicus between God and you through which you get all your sustenance. Whatever Mahatmas and Lords there may be in the universe can be nothing more than midwives at your spiritual birth, which is a continuous performance. The more Masters and Mahatmas and Lords you find in creation, the farther away from God you will be in consciousness. Wipe them off the map! Make your own at-one-ment with God, just as the Mahatmas and Lords claim to do. This doesn't mean that you cannot learn anything from any school teacher, or Mahatma, or Lord, or whatever other instructors there may be in the world. You can learn things from sticks and stones and running brooks.

The teachers in the temple learned from a twelve-year-old child, and I HAVE been clear-seeing enough to learn things from a one-year-old child. There are times and occasions when you can learn very much more from a baby than you can from the oldest Mahatma that ever posed. Don't despise the child and worship the

84

Mahatma. Don't stumble over the sticks and fall into the brooks while you are gazing adoringly at some self-styled "Master."

Don't believe everything you hear from persons who pretend to high places and superior knowledge.

They may be pretending and they may not.

But in either event they can pass on to you none of the wisdom which God has passed on to them.

Believe only the wisdom which God gives you in the sanctuary of your own heart and mind. In other words, do your own thinking and discovering, touch God for yourself and believe in the wisdom that God gives you in preference to accepting cock-and-bull stories from other people who pretend to be in closer touch with God than you are. Nobody is any closer to God than you are.

Nobody is dearer to God than you are. Nobody has any more of a monopoly of God than you have.

See that nobody has any greater faith in the God within him than you have. See that nobody depends more absolutely upon the God within him than you depend upon the God within you. Do the will of God within you, and you shall know what to believe on all manner of subjects.

Remember that God is All-Wisdom, All-Power, and All-Presence; that he is all these things in every pin point of space in this universe; that he is all these things within you, for you to use, to confide in, to act upon. Be still and know God.

Trust no authority but the authority if your own heart and mind, which is the heart and mind of God. So shall you grow in consciousness of the One God which is your real self and power and wisdom as it is every other man's real self and power and wisdom. Call no man Master, call no teacher Master, call no Mahatma Master, call no Lord Master.

Only One is your Master, the One within you.

Made in the USA
Middletown, DE
10 November 2018